ACHIEVING BUSINESS EXCELLENCE

by Pravin Rajpal

Om Books International, India

ACHIEVING BUSINESS EXCELLENCE

by Pravin Rajpal

Published by

Om Books International
4379/4B, Prakash House, Ansari Road,
Daryaganj, New Delhi-110002
Tel : 91-11-23263363, 23265303
Fax : 91-11-23278091
E-mail : sales@ombooks.com
Website : www.ombooks.com

Edited by : Sonalini Dawar

Designed by : Creative Concepts

Printed in India

ISBN-10 : 81-87108-27-4
ISBN-13 : 978-81-87108-27-6

CONTENTS

PRODUCTS & PROCESSES 211-322

QUALITY 323-390

INNOVATION 391-462

1

Business Excellence

"Outstanding people have one thing in common:- An absolute sense of MISSION."

Zig Ziglar

"The greatest danger for most of us is not that our aim is too high and we miss it, but that it is too low and we reach it."

Michelangelo

"I have offended God and mankind because my work didn't reach the quality it should have."

Leonardo-da-Vinci

Italian painter, sculptor, architect and engineer - A genius, often referred as 'Renaissance man'.(A man who excels in various fields.) The greatest painter of all times.

The secret of 'Excellence' is contained in one word – 'Passion'.
If you are passionate about your work, you will always enjoy it.
If you enjoy what you do, you will EXCEL.

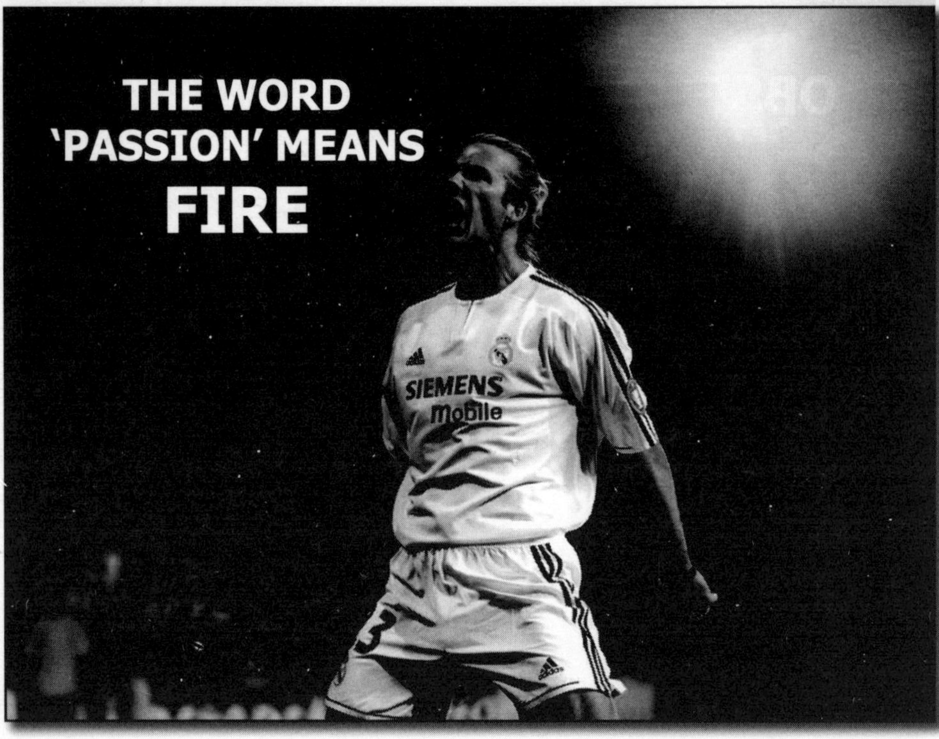
THE WORD
'PASSION' MEANS
FIRE
SIEMENS
Mobile

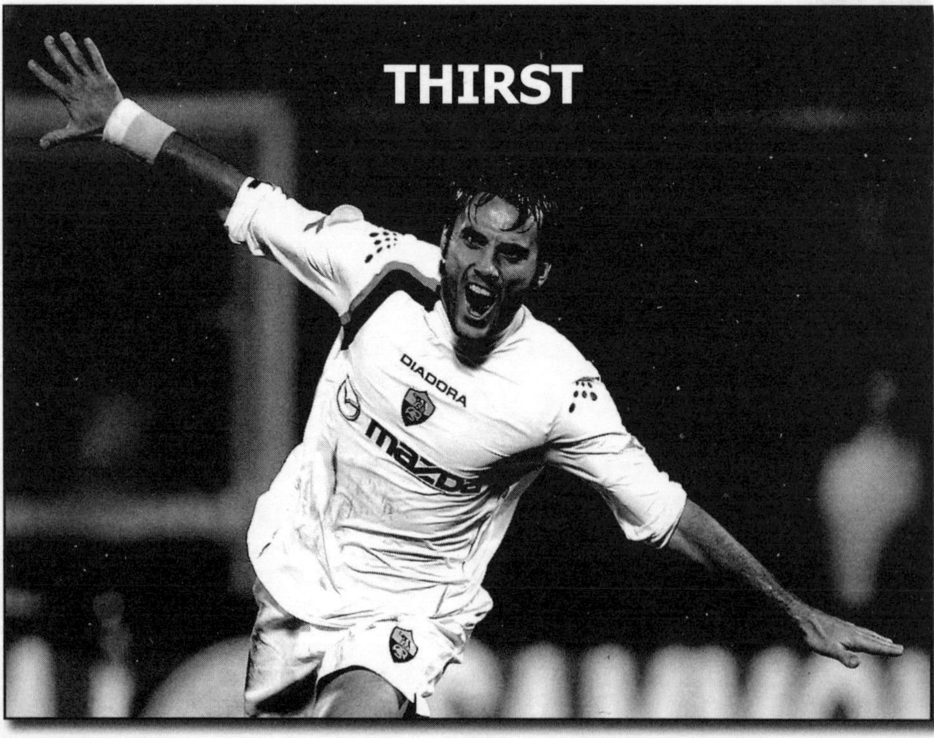
THIRST
DIADORA
mazda

OBSESSION

AND CRAVING.

IT IS INTENSE,

HIGH-WROUGHT
EMOTION

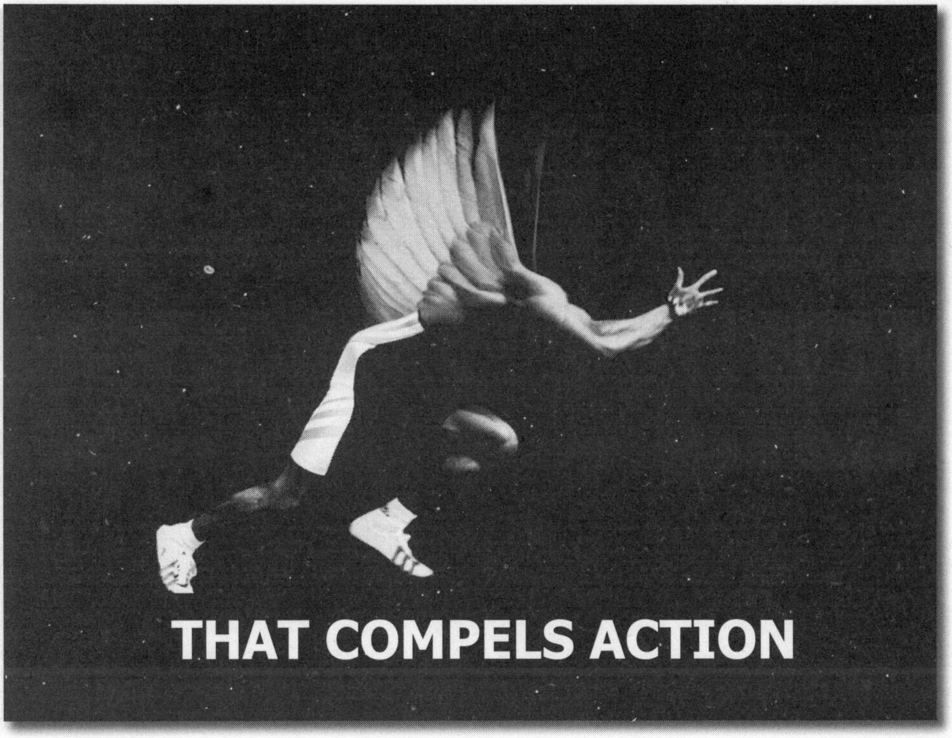
THAT COMPELS ACTION

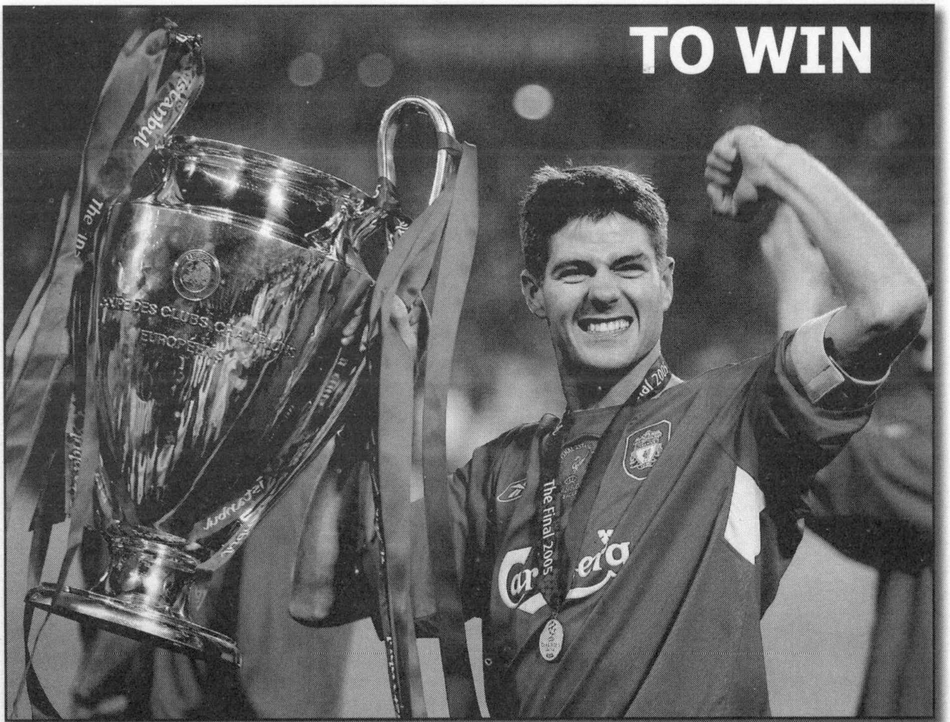
TO WIN
The Final 2005
Carlsberg

The Need for Business Excellence

- We live in a world, where today's breakthrough product is tomorrow's undifferentiated commodity. Customer expectations, needs and demands are changing overnight. They are demanding more than ever before and will not settle for any thing less than the 'best' or 'excellent'. They continuously demand excellent quality, great designs, new features, WOW factors and innovation. For getting all these, they want to spend lesser money, time and efforts.
- New benchmarks for excellence are set up and even surpassed everyday. There is one big question, which every one is asking today - "How do we meet these challenges?"
- **The answer is 'Business Excellence' – We don't have any other choice!**

Business Excellence

'Business Excellence' is a relative and dynamic concept. It means exceeding any competitor on:

- **Innovation**
- **Product quality**
- **Cost competitiveness**
- **Delivery**
- **Customer satisfaction**
- **Service**

'Excellence' - A Dynamic Concept

Since 'Business Excellence' is a comparative term, it always refers to excellent performance in relation to:

- Competitors and
- Accepted international business excellence awards:
  - European Foundation for Quality Management (EFQM)*
  - Malcolm Baldrige Quality Award*

***Explained in the following chapters.**

Fundamental Concepts of Business Excellence...

Leadership

Visionary and inspirational leadership, coupled with clear directions & constancy of purpose.

Continuous Improvement & Innovation

Challenging the status-quo for and effecting change by using learning to create innovation and improvement opportunities.

Customer Focus

Creating sustainable customer value and exceeding their expectations.

Achieving results that delight all the organization's stakeholders.

Inspiring High Performance

Maximizing the contribution of employees through their development and involvement.

Partnership Development

Developing and maintaining value-adding partnerships with all the stakeholders.

Impact on Society

Strive to understand and respond to the expectations of the society at large.

European Foundation for Quality Management (EFQM)

Business Excellence Award Framework

European Foundation for Quality Management

The EFQM Excellence Model was introduced at the beginning of 1992 as the framework for assessing organizations for the European Quality Award. It is now the most widely used organizational framework in Europe and has become the basis for the majority of national and regional Quality Awards. The award is the **benchmark for business excellence.**

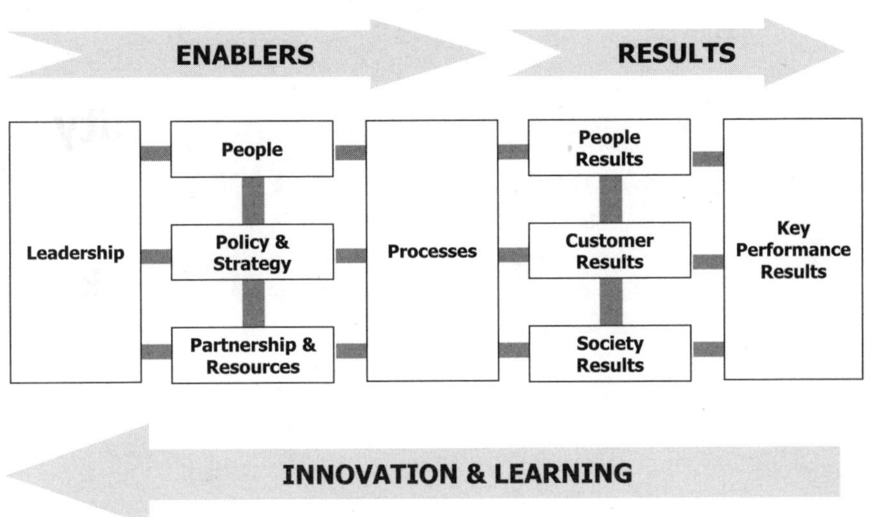

Enablers & Results

The EFQM Excellence Model is based on 9 criteria:

- Five of these are **'Enablers'** and four are **'Results'.**
- The 'Enablers' criteria cover what an organization does.
- The 'Results' criteria cover what an organization achieves.
- 'Results' are caused by 'Enablers'.
- 'Enablers' are improved by using the feedback from 'Results'.

Dynamic Model

Excellent results with respect to Performance, Customers, People and Society are achieved through Leadership driving Policy and Strategy, that is delivered through People, Partnerships and Processes.

The model gives lot of importance to innovation and learning for sustainable advantages. It shows how the innovation and learning can impact the 'Enablers' for maximizing the 'Results'.

EFQM Excellence Model

The model serves as:

- A tool for setting **right directions** for business excellence.
- A way to benchmark with other organizations.
- A guide to identify areas for improvement.
- A structure for the organization's management system.

Malcolm Baldrige Quality Award & Performance Excellence Framework

Malcolm Baldrige Quality Award

The award was established by the U.S Congress in 1987 to raise awareness of quality management and recognize U.S companies that have successfully implemented quality management.

The U.S commerce department's National Institute of Standards & Technology (NIST) manages the award and the American Society for Quality (ASQ) administers it.

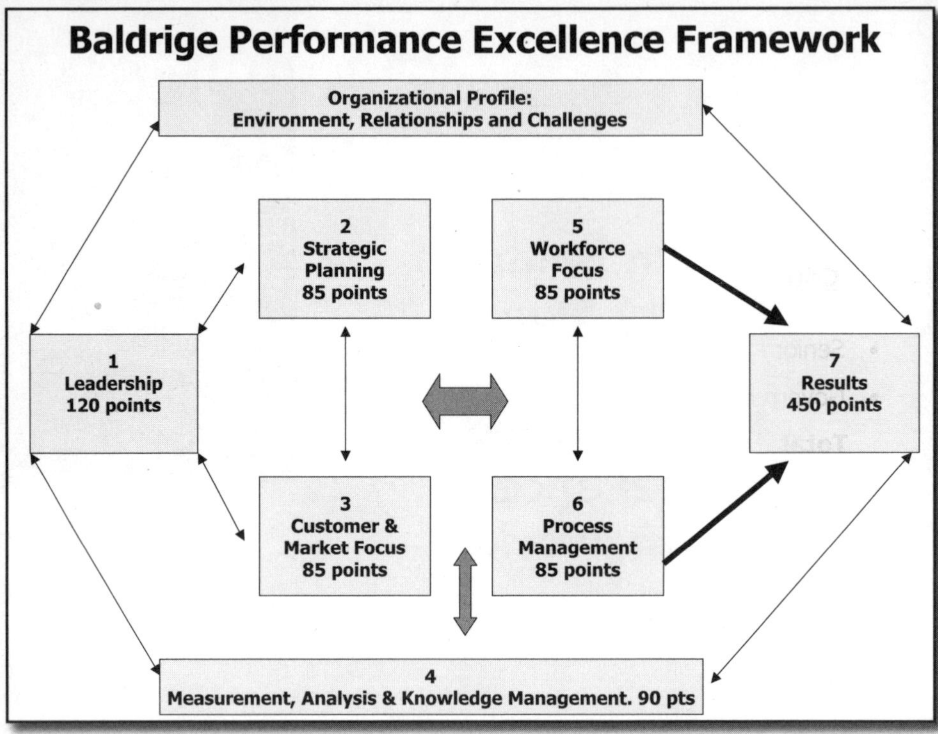

Award - Framework

Malcolm Baldrige Quality Award framework symbolizes the highest standards of quality. It is a benchmark for business excellence. The award is evaluated on the basis of 1000 points and is divided in 7 main criteria as shown in the above diagram.

The break-up of the points and key parameters are shown below.

1. Leadership

Criteria	Points
• Senior executive leadership	70
• Governance & social responsibilities	50
Total	**120**

Leadership
Key Parameters

- Vision & values.
- Legal & ethical behaviour.
- Creating sustainable organization.
- Communicating with entire workforce.
- Fiscal accountability.
- Accountability for management's actions.
- Transparency in operations.
- Impact on society.
- Supporting key communities.

2. Strategic Quality Planning

Criteria	Points
• Strategy development	40
• Strategy deployment	45
Total	**85**

Strategic Quality Planning
Key Parameters

- Organization's strengths, weaknesses, opportunities & threats.
- Long term organizational sustainability.
- Important goals.
- Strategic objectives.
- Points of differentiation.
- Balancing short-term and long-term challenges & opportunities.
- Providing adequate financial & other resources.
- Deployment of policy effectively.
- Key performance indicators.
- Comparisons with key competitors.

3. Customer & Market Focus

Criteria	Points
• Customer & market knowledge	40
• Customer relationship & satisfaction	45
Total	**85**

Customer & Market Focus
Key Parameters

- Identification of customers, customer groups and market segments.
- Current and future customer needs determination.
- Using customer's voice for new products.
- Remaining sensitive to dynamic forces.
- Customer relationship management.
- Key access mechanisms.
- Customer satisfaction determination.
- Using vital customer information for improvement.

4. Measurement, Analysis & Knowledge Management

Criteria	Points
• Measurement analysis and improvement	45
• Management of information, I.T & knowledge	45
Total	**90**

Measurement, Analysis & Knowledge...
Key Parameters

- Collection, alignment and integration of performance related data.
- Review of performance and capabilities.
- Evaluation of competitive performance.
- Translation of performance findings for continuous and breakthrough improvements.
- Providing valuable information to workforce, suppliers, partners, collaborators and customers.
- Hardware and software capabilities.
- Accuracy and reliability of information.
- Timeliness, security and confidentiality of valuable information.
- Transfer of information from and to customers & workforce.

5. Workforce Focus

Criteria	Points
• Workforce engagement	45
• Workforce environment	40
Total	**85**

Workforce Focus
Key Parameters

- Effective workforce engagement.
- Fostering culture of high-performance.
- Goal setting, empowerment and initiative.
- Innovation in work environment.
- Leveraging from diverse ideas, cultures and thinking.
- Workforce leadership development.
- Development of organization knowledge.
- Core competencies and action plans.
- Managing effective career progression.
- Workforce motivation and retention.
- Workplace health, safety and security.

6. Process Management

Criteria	Points
• Work systems design	35
• Work process management & improvement	50
Total	**85**

Process Management
Key Parameters

- Core competencies.
- Key work processes.
- How the processes deliver customer value, profitability, success and sustainability.
- Emergency readiness.
- Key performance measures of the processes.
- Application of process application tools and techniques.

7. Results

Criteria	Points
• Product & service outcomes	100
• Customer focused outcomes	70
• Financial & market outcomes	70
• Workforce focused results	70
• Process effectiveness outcomes	70
• Leadership outcomes	70
Total	**450**

Results
Key Parameters

- Product levels and trends.
- Customer satisfaction levels and comparisons with competitors.
- Industry standing.
- Market share and growth.
- Financial results and growth.
- Workforce satisfaction.
- Process productivity, cycle-time etc.
- Fiscal accountability.

Core Values of 'Baldrige Performance Excellence'

The criteria are built on the following set of inter-related core values:

- Visionary leadership
- Customer-driven excellence
- Organizational and personal learning
- Valuing employees and partners
- Agility
- **Focus on the future**
- Managing for innovation
- Management by fact
- Social responsibility
- Focus on results and creating value
- Systems perspective

Foresight - Insight - Action

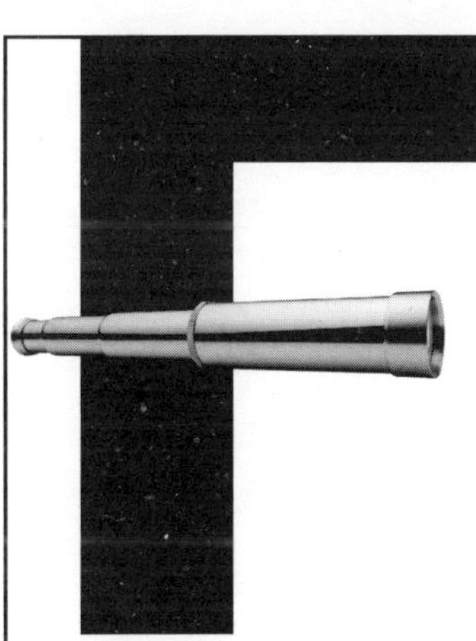

Focus on Future

One of the core values of 'Malcolm Baldrige Business Excellence Framework' is to **focus on future**. Creating a sustainable organization requires understanding the short and long-term factors that affect your organization and market-place. Pursuit of sustainable growth and **market leadership** requires a strong future orientation.

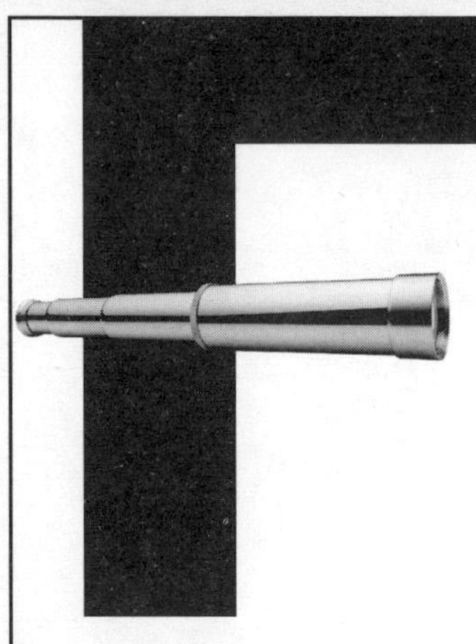

Future Trends

The organization's planning should anticipate many factors like future business trends, upcoming markets, new business and partnering opportunities, technological developments, changes in customer and market segments, evolving regulatory requirements and strategic moves by the competitors.

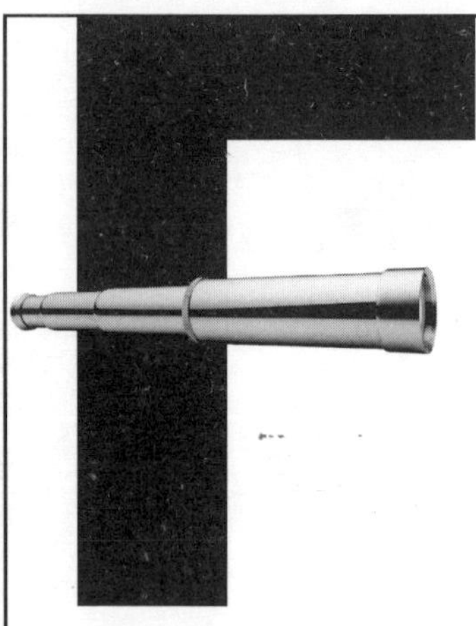

Requirements

A strong future orientation requires:

1. **Foresight -** Ability of predicting the future trends.
2. **Insight -** Good understanding of customer needs.
3. **Action -** World class execution.

1 Foresight

"Business, more than any other occupation, is a continual dealing with the future; it is a continual calculation, an instinctive exercise in foresight."

Henri R.Luce

Predicting the Future

In an age of uncertainty, peering **10 years into the future** may seem to be a challenging task, but ignoring long-term demographic, economic and corporate trends is an even less attractive option.

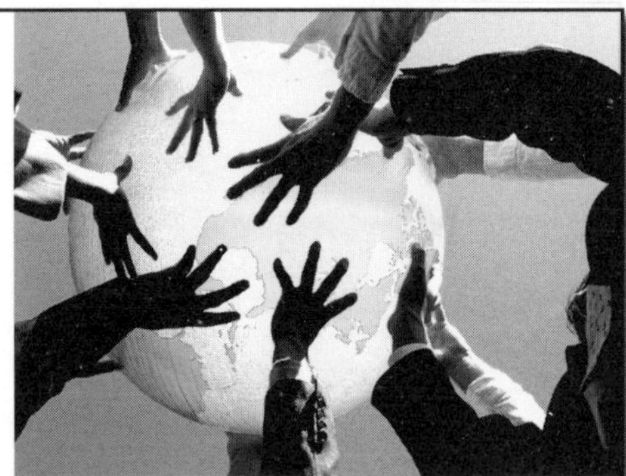

Globalization

- Globalization will remain the major trend for the next 10 years. Emerging markets, **China and India** in particular, will take a greater slice of the world economy.
- There will be a greater degree of convergence of patterns of production, consumption, price, salaries, interest rates and profits.
- There will also be a greater economic inter-dependence of countries world-wide, resulting in lot of new business opportunities.

Innovations

- New products, new methods of production, opening of new markets and new sources of supplies will assume great importance for sustaining competitive advantages.
- Besides new products, innovations will be about new business models, marketplace collaboration and new designs. The pace of innovation will be much faster. As new innovations take place, the shelf-life of the products will become even shorter.

Knowledge Management

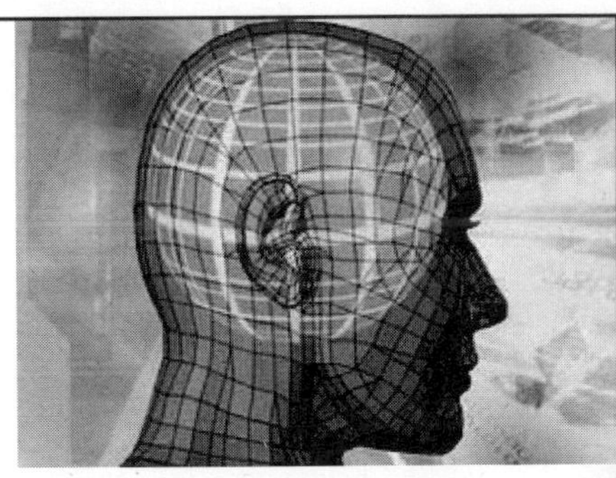

Since, the focus of management attention will be on the areas of innovation, the next decade belongs to 'knowledge capital'. The ability to develop and retain the intellectual capital will play a decisive role in the future success of the organizations. The knowledge worker will have to focus on the following important areas:

- Achieving shorter new product development cycles.
- Increasing the responsiveness to external environment.
- Leveraging from global networks.

Demographics Based

Population shifts will have a significant impact on economies, companies and customers. World population will rise to 8 billion from the present 6 billion, with **India and China having 40%** of the world's consumer market. According to United Nations, the total share of Europe's population will come down to merely 7% of the total world population in 2050.

Personalization

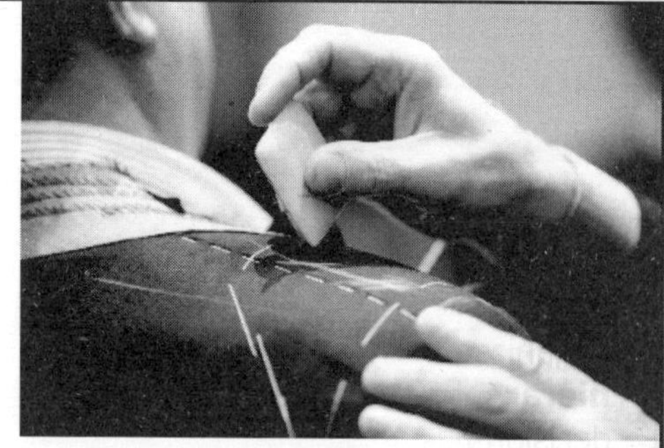

Demands from the customers will be ever increasing. Price and quality will matter as much as ever, but developing markets will place more emphasis on **personalization and customization.** This is particularly applicable to the service industries like banks and insurance companies, who will have to tailor make their services in accordance with the specific requirements of their customers.

Specialization

- Processes will be **outsourced or off-shored** in accordance with wherever they are done best. Organizations will try to focus their energies on core competencies and leave their non-core functions to other enterprises for cost-effectiveness.
- This will open up plenty of new business opportunities for specialized functions like information technology, human resources, marketing, manufacturing, engineering, real estate management, accounting and many other customer support activities.

Freedom

Organizations will become **flatter and less hierarchical.** Employees will be given greater decision-making autonomy and will participate more actively in developing new products and services. There will be a lot of freedom with accountability.

Integration

Business and technology will fuse into one system, one conversation, one strategy, for **one world.** This is central to understanding the **New Future.**

2. Insight
Emerging Trends & Opportunities

Spending Power

Indians have greater spending power today than they have ever had before. With the income on the rise, the spending is on the rise too. According to a survey done by Hewitt Associates, the rise in the Indian salaries was about 14% during 2006-07, which is the highest in the Asian region.

Retail

India is ranked at the **number one** position in the emerging retail markets of the world. India is followed by Russia, China, Vietnam, Ukraine & Chile. India has retained the top position for three consecutive years – 2005, 2006 & 2007.

Source - A.T Kearney survey.

Food

According to Euromonitor International, a market research company, the amount of money Indians spend on meals outside the home has more than **doubled** in the past decade.

Indians spend about USD 5 billion a year on outside meals and the amount is expected to double again in about 5 years time.

Bio-tech

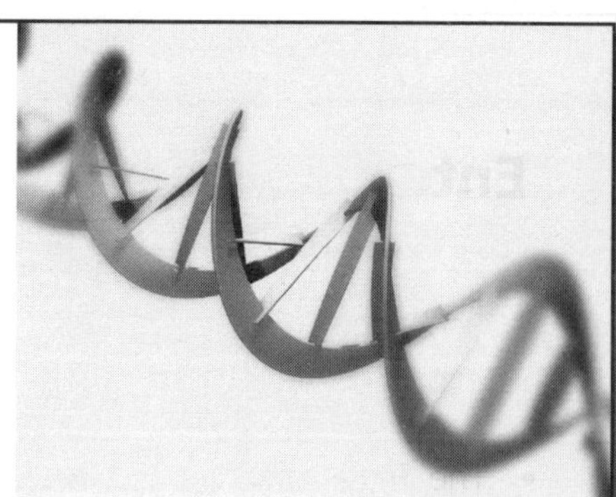

An Ernst and Young study has named India as one of the **five emerging biotech leaders** in the Asia Pacific followed by Singapore, China and Japan. Large number of emerging sectors are discovering plenty of advantages with the cost-effective, young and well educated work-force of India.

Automobiles

- India became **the fastest growing car market** in the world in 2004, with a growth rate of 20 per cent. India added 1.5 million new cars during 2006-07.
- India is ranked as the 2nd largest two-wheeler market and 4th largest commercial vehicles market in the world.
- India is also a booming auto component industry. 40% of the global auto component industry is expected to be sourced from India.

Entertainment

- The Indian film industry is said to be one of the **largest in the world**.
- India is the **3rd largest television** market in the world today.
- Entertainment ranks very high on the spending index of the Indians.
- The media and entertainment sector is passing through the golden era.
- India makes about 1000 films every year.
- Animation and special effects business is expected to go up very rapidly in the near future.

Real-Estate

- The real-estate in India is booming.
- India is ranked 5th **in the list of 30 emerging markets by** the global real-estate consulting group Knight Frank and they have predicted an impressive 20 per cent growth rate for the organized retail segment by 2010.

Information Technology

- India has emerged as the **fastest growing information technology hub in the world.** The software Industry continues to remain India's sunshine sector.
- In the software industry, India is a knowledge hub for custom application development, system integration, IT consulting, application management, service oriented architecture and web enabled services.
- When it comes to IT enabled services – the whole world looks at India. The IT sector has grown **10 times** in the last decade and is expected to maintain the same pace.

Tourism & Hospitality

According to exclusive research by the World Travel and Tourism Council (WTTC), India is one of the fastest growing tourism economies in the world today. India is ranked as the **4th most attractive destination** in the world after Italy, New Zealand and Australia. India is visited by about 4 million tourists every year.

Telecommunications

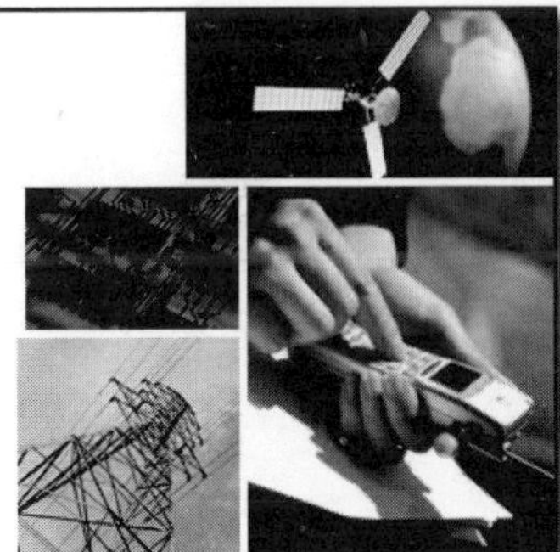

- India is the 3rd largest mobile phone users market in the world after China and USA.
- One of the **fastest growing sectors** in the country, telecommunications has been zooming up at a very fast pace during the past few years.
- India adds 6 million mobile subscribers every month and has the total user base of 200 million subscribers. This figure is expected to touch the 400 million mark by 2010.

Summary

India is on a take-off stage. The country stands on the threshold of unprecedented growth and is well established as a:

- **Consumer powerhouse**
- **Knowledge hub**
- **Preferred investment destination**

3. Action

First excellence principle of Tom Peters:-

"A strong bias for ACTION."

"Never forget implementation. In our work it's what I call the missing 98 percent of the client puzzle."

Al McDonald / McKinsey

"The truth of the matter is that there is nothing you can't accomplish if:

- You clearly decide what is it, that you are absolutely committed to achieving.
- You are willing to take **massive action.**
- You notice what is working or not working.
- You continue to change your approach until you achieve what you want, using whatever is given along the way."

Anthony Robbins

"It gets back to planning versus acting:
We act from day one;
others plan 'how to plan' for months."

Bloomberg

Steps for Result Oriented Approach

I. SMART Goals

S Specific
M Measurable
A Agreed upon
R Realistic
T Time-based

Examples

- 100 stores, 100 cities, 100 months
- 50,000 cars in 12 months
- 60% market share by 2010

Specific

- Well defined
- Clear to all

Measurable

In terms of:

- **Cost**
- **Time**
- **Deliverables**

Agreed Upon

Agreement with all the stakeholders.

Realistic

Within the availability of:

- **Resources**
- **Knowledge**
- **Time**

Time Based

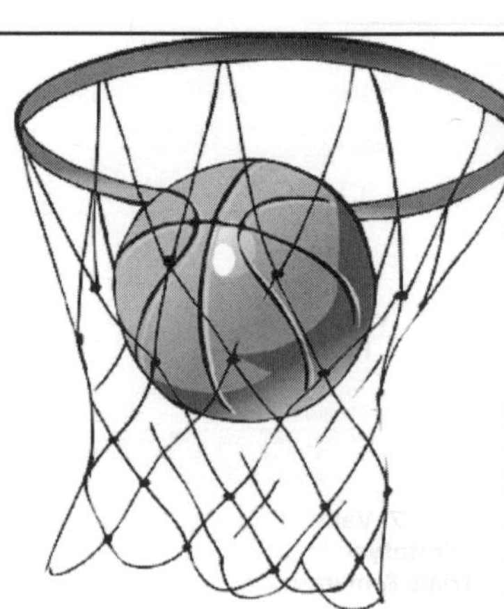

- **Enough time to achieve the goals.**
- **Not too much time, which can affect project performance adversely.**

II. Cycle-time Reduction

Time is not infinite and limitless. Competing on the basis of time has the following advantages:

- Maximizing competitive advantages.
- Identifying market opportunities.
- Responding to those opportunities before the competitors.

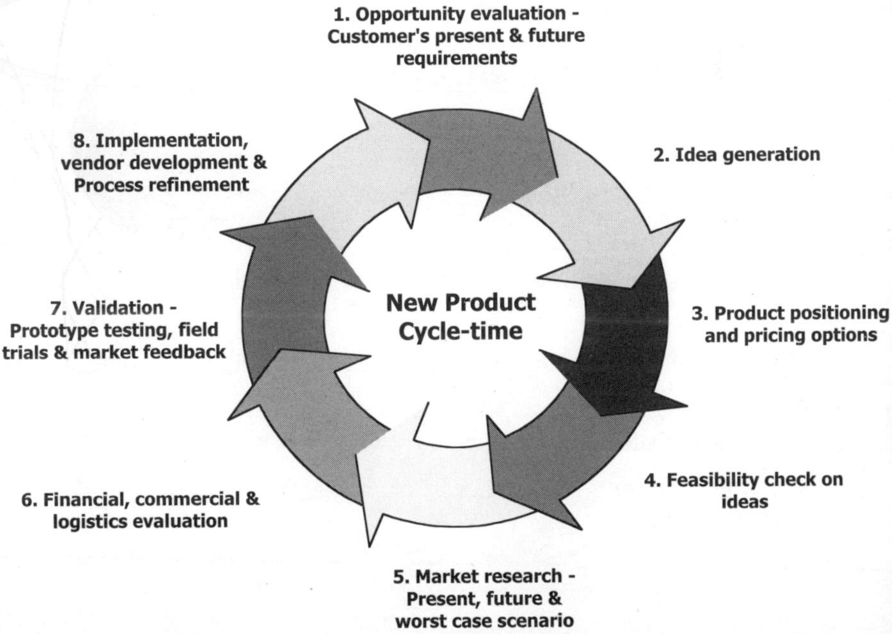

III. Risk Management

Risk Management

- The solution to fast action is informed and calculated risk taking.
- Risk can be defined as the **probability** of occurrence of an undesirable event and the impact / consequences of that event.
- Risk management is a process of managing risk by using risk abatement plans.

Objectives of Risk Management Plan

- To identify and quantify risk elements viz. **technical, cost, marketing risk etc.**
- To reduce the risk by means of risk abatement plans.
- To monitor the progress of risk abatement plans.
- To highlight and manage the risk as early as possible.

Key Steps of a Risk Management Process

- Identify risk elements and risk types.
- Assign risk ratings.
- Prioritize risk as high, medium and low.
- Identify risk abatement plans for high and medium risks.
- Incorporate the risk abatement plans into work plans.

Methods of Risk Abatement

- Involve customers, suppliers and dealers early in the process.
- Ensure good value propositions for the customers.
- Calculate the best, most likely and worst case scenarios.
- Conduct proper market tests before marketing the products.
- Conduct periodic project review.

IV. Project Management

Project Management

Project management can be summarized in a triangle. The three most important factors are:

- **Schedule**
- **Cost**
- **Performance**

Project Management...

1. Projects must be delivered **on time.**
2. Projects must be **within cost.**
3. Projects must meet customer's **performance requirements.**

Note: These points will be covered extensively in next sections.

Paradigm Shift

In their journey to business excellence, people must break away from the following paradigms or mind-sets:

From
Profits
to
Competitive Advantages

Profit is the outcome of sustained competitive advantages and not vice-versa. The goal of the organization must be to maximize the competitive advantages in price, quality, delivery & innovation.

From

Customer Satisfaction

to

Great Customer Experience

Satisfaction is not good enough. Customers look for excellence everywhere. They will not settle for anything less than the best and demand excellence in performance, features, designs, innovations & services – All these for lesser cost, efforts and time.

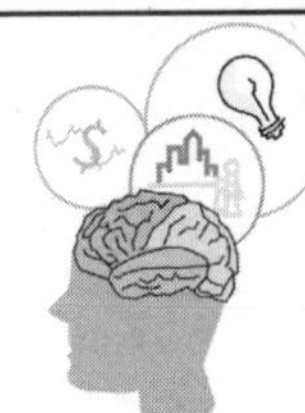

From

Zero Defects

to

Zero Customer Problems

A defect is only one of the customer problems. A defect free product may still have too many other customer problems in installation, servicing, maintenance, after sales support & training. The goal of the organization should be 'Zero customer problems'.

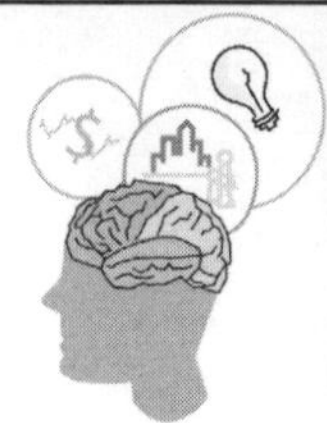

From
Controlling Costs
to
Maximizing Revenues

Costs can be controlled up to a certain limit. Market expansion and diversification is limitless. Organizations must apply their resources in building new markets and diversification. They must strive to develop a good range of products for various customers and focus on maximizing sales.

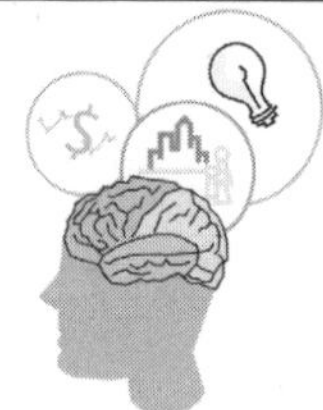

From
Financial Costs
to
Opportunity Costs

Opportunity cost of lost customers, lost business opportunity, loss of first mover advantages and lost time prove to be more costly in the long run. Delays in executing new projects result in delays in revenues. In business, time is more important than money.

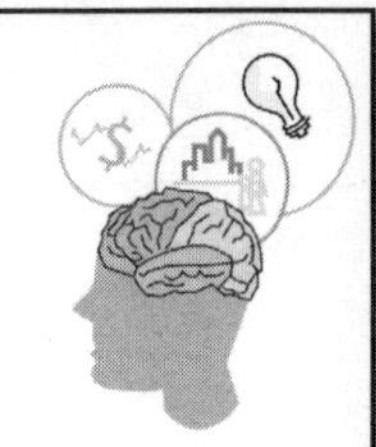

From
WYSWYG
'What You See is, What You Get'
to
WYGWYG
'What You Give is, What You Get'

If you act in an ordinary manner, you get ordinary results; Act reasonably well and you get reasonable results; Act extra-ordinarily and you get extra-ordinary results. 'What you give is what you get', The rule applies to your employees, products, customers and everywhere universally.

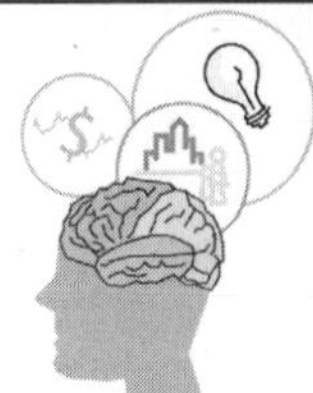

From
Competition as a 'THREAT'
to
Competition as an 'OPPORTUNITY'

Every competitor is a potential business partner. Look for synergies. Every organization has unique strengths which can be combined for added customer values.

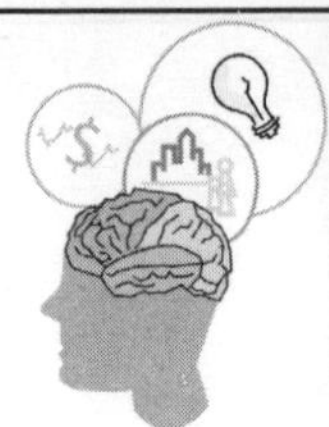

From Stated Needs to Unperceived & Unarticulated Needs

Stated needs already have a lot of competition in the market. Organizations must strive to translate the unperceived and unarticulated customer needs into development of new products for becoming the market leaders.

Functionality is mundane. Great designs emote desirability. Organizations must make products with irresistible designs to sustain the competitive advantages.

From
Planning
to
Action

Today's dynamic and turbulent markets require fast action. Organizations waste too much time in the planning activities. They must act fast to stay ahead. They must strive for having the first advantages. Act fast – act right now to outperform your competitors.

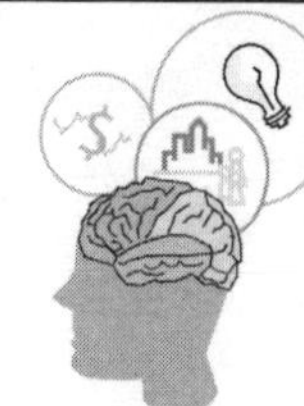

From
Best is the 'End Point'
to
Best is the 'Starting Point'

'Best' is not good enough. Start from the 'best' and expand in unexpected ways by applying various permutations and combinations for achieving excellence.

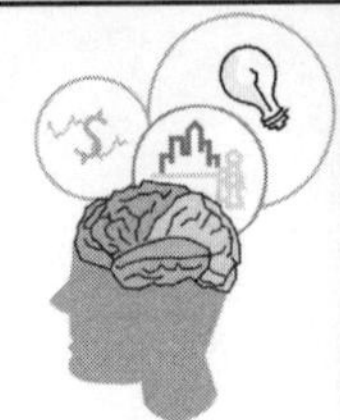

From
Conventional Wisdom
to
Un-conventional Wisdom

People must challenge the existing business models with unconventional wisdom. Re-invent, re-imagine and re-discover new business models for unprecedented success.

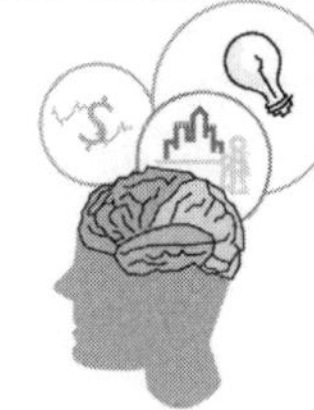

From
Professionals
to
Passionate People

Get the passionate people to work for your organization. They will always surprise you with their performance. There are no obstacles for passionate people. They are determined, focused and hungry for success.

From
Innovation is Tough
to
Innovation is Easy!

Innovation is easy. It is a process. Start generating new ideas from the customer's problems. Quite often innovation is the result of connecting different products, organizations, suppliers, technologies & disciplines.

From
Punish Failures
to
Fail to Succeed

Each failure is a step forward to success. It teaches very important lessons. It is important to make the course correction and move ahead. Organizations must allow their people to experiment, fail, learn but finally succeed. Success with new products and services is very often the result of trial and error.

From
Quality
to
Innovation

Quality has become the minimum performance criteria of a product. Too many organizations chasing each rupee or dollar of consumer spending has already resulted in market share erosion for many players. Organizations must strive to innovate new products and services to remain the market leaders.

From
'Mediocrity'
to
'Excellence'

'Mediocrity' is passé. Organizations must strive for 'EXCELLENCE' in whatever they do. They must inspire their people to produce excellent work, have excellent processes and provide excellent products and services to their customers.

Business Excellence Assessment Score Sheet

This assessment score sheet contains 70 questions divided into following sections:

1. **Leadership**
2. **Strategic Planning**
3. **Information**
4. **Human Resource Focus**
5. **Customers**
6. **Suppliers**
7. **Processes**
8. **Impact on Society**
9. **Business Results**

NOTE: All questions must be answered on a 1 to 5 scale.
(1 is the lowest and 5 is the highest)

1. Leadership

		Score
1	Is the top management having personal visible involvement in all aspects of quality management?	
2	Do they actively participate in creating and re-inforcing customer focus throughout the organization?	
3	Do they provide full support by providing appropriate resources?	
4	Do they actively involve themselves in recognizing the employee/ team contributions?	
	TOTAL	

2. Strategic Planning

		Score
5	Does the company have a common vision which is shared by all the employees in its true sense?	
6	Does the company's strategic planning address re-alignment of work processes to improve customer focus and operational performance?	
7	Are the company's strategies targeted for quantified measurable improvement in important areas and is building for future seen as more important than short-term benefits?	
8	Is commitment to resources for new facilities, process improvements and training done considering long-term objectives?	
9	Does the company's long term projections of operational performance effectively incorporate comparisons with competitors?	
	TOTAL	

3. Information

		Score
10	Is the company updated with the latest trends in information management / technology?	
11	Do the employees feel free to share information?	
12	Is the company's information management system accessible to every one without any difficulty?	
13	Does the company periodically update its information management system?	
14	Is the information system reliable and accurate for people to make decisions in time?	
	TOTAL	

4. Human Resource Focus

		Score
15	Is there a quality culture in the organization?	
16	Does the company follow strong value systems?	
17	Is every one trained in the organization to follow ethical practices?	
18	Does the company have an effective system for setting both quantitative and qualitative targets?	
19	Are the employees generally aware and meet the expected performance standards?	
20	Does the company make efforts to integrate employee's job performance with key quality improvement targets and business results?	
21	Does the company have an effective appraisal system which takes care of the career progression of all the employees?	
22	Does the company promote creativity & innovation and encourage employees for 'out-of-the-box' thinking?	
23	Is there a system for employee recognition?	
24	Is the employee motivation level high and good performance suitably rewarded?	
25	Does the company analyze reasons for employee exit and is the employee turnover ratio kept to the minimum?	
26	Is every one in the organization given training on time management & stress management so that they carry out the company's task in the productive manner?	
27	Is the company able to attract the best talent?	
	TOTAL	

5. Customers

		Score
28	Is every one in the organization trained to meet the expectations of the internal and external customers?	
29	Are the customers very satisfied with the company's products and services?	
30	Do the customers come back for repeat purchases?	
31	Do the products enjoy a competitive edge over nearest competitors?	
32	Does the company regularly improve their products through PDCA to meet their customer expectations?	
33	Does the company promptly resolve all formal and informal customer complaints?	
34	Does the company regularly determine customer's current and expected requirements?	
35	Does the company determine specific product feature and their relative importance using customer listening techniques like QFD?	
36	Does the company analyze and use information on customer loss / gain and product performance to innovate new products / services?	
37	Does the company effectively determine customer satisfaction and make efforts to improve it further?	
38	Does the company involve customers in innovating new products / services?	
39	Is the customer satisfaction level effectively compared with that of your key competitors by in-house studies and independent surveys?	
40	Does the company improve its system of determining customer satisfaction on a regular basis?	
41	Does the company effectively use customer dissatisfaction indicators for making improvements?	
42	Has the company achieved better market share for its products and services in relation to key competitors?	
	TOTAL	

6. Suppliers

		Score
43	Does the company evaluate supplier performance with specified requirements / parameters through mutually agreed plans?	
44	Does the company effectively communicate its quality requirements to the suppliers?	
45	Does the company effectively evaluate if suppliers are meeting the quality requirements?	
46	Does the company organize training programs for the suppliers to improve their capabilities and response times?	
47	Does the company have a system to generate healthy competition among suppliers of similar items to improve performance?	
48	What is the level of supplier satisfaction?	
49	Are the suppliers paid in time?	
50	Does the company involve suppliers for innovation?	
	TOTAL	

7. Processes

		Score
51	Is 'Quality' the main objective of all the manufacturing processes?	
52	Does the company validate its product designs taking into account performance, process and supplier capabilities?	
53	Does the company regularly determine waste / non-value-adding activities from the system and eliminates them to improve efficiency?	
54	Does the company determine the cause of variation, make corrections and integrate them into the processes?	
55	Does the company regularly analyze the quality costs and ensure that maximum focus is given to preventive measures?	
56	Does the company regularly improve key business processes, their requirements, quality and operational performance?	
57	Does the company regularly improve its manufactuiring processes by application of scientific techniques like 5S, TPM, Gemba Kaizen & PDCA?	
58	Does the company effectively use JIT and LEAN principles for improving operating efficiency?	
59	Does the company effectively deploy mistake proofing techniques to improve its overall manufacturing processes?	
60	Does the company make efforts to find out information from best-in-class and make use of this information for process improvement?	
61	Does the company innovate new processes for cutting down cycle times?	
62	Does the company's work culture ensure that there is continuous improvement in the product quality based on customer needs & expectations?	
63	Has the company introduced a system of quality MIS to ensure that the organization is continuously looking for opportunities for improvement?	
	TOTAL	

8. Impact on Society

		Score
64	Is the company effectively satisfying the needs and expectations of the society at large?	
65	Does the company effectively evaluate possible impact of its products and operations on society?	
66	Does the company promote ethical conduct in all the activities? Are company's advertisement campaigns truthful?	
67	Does the company effectively consider energy conservation and preservation of global resources?	
	TOTAL	

9. Business Results

		Score
68	Has the company significantly improved its market share from the previous year?	
69	Is the company's growth over the last financial year comparable with the industry growth?	
70	Are the overall financial results better than the last financial year and have the shareholders' expectations been met?	
	TOTAL	

GRAND TOTAL (Total of all sheets from section 1 to 9)

Analyze your score:

0-140 **Serious situation**

141-210 **Average**

211-280 **Good**

281-350 **Excellent - There is no room for complacency. Keep it up.**

2

Leadership

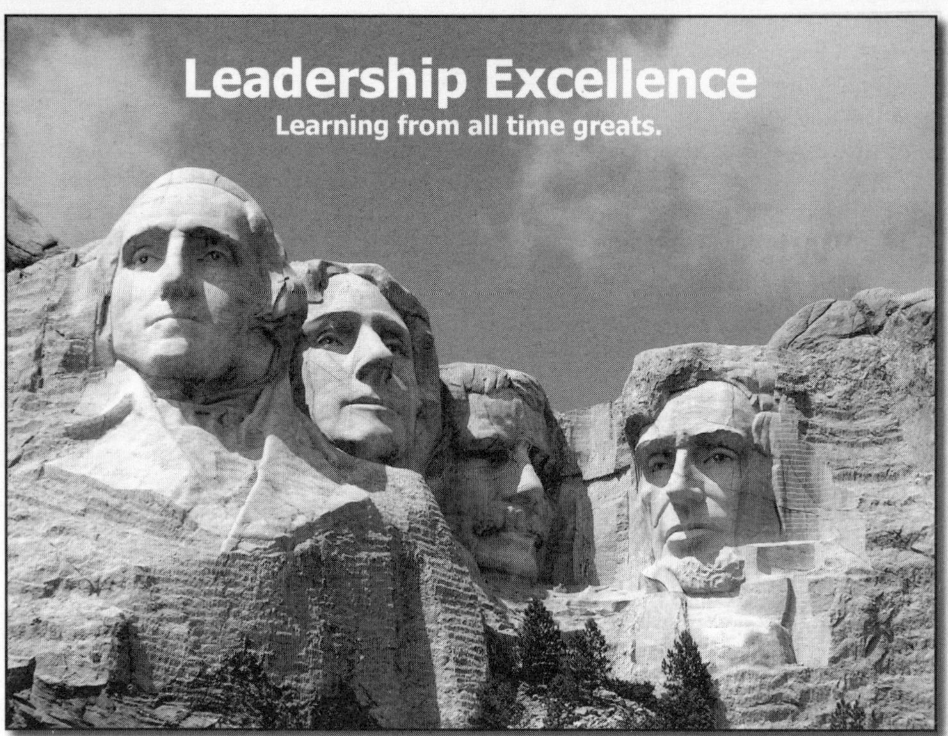

"I start with the premise that the function of leadership is to produce more leaders, not more followers."

Ralph Nader

"Whatever action is performed by a great man, common men follow in his footsteps and whatever standards he sets by exemplary acts, all the world pursues."

Bhagawad Gita

"Not armies, not nations, have advanced the race; but here and there in the course of ages, a leader has stood up and cast his shadow over the world."

Edwin H. Chapin

"Leadership is a privilege to better the lives of others. It is not an opportunity to satisfy the personal greed."

Mwai Kibaki

"Leadership is ACTION, not position."

Donald H. McGannon

"Leaders must inspire people of this generation to do things that surpass and exceed all other generations of the past, in all the things that make life worth living."

W.White

"Never tell a young person that something can not be done. God may have been waiting for centuries for somebody ignorant enough of the impossible to do that thing."

John Andrew Holmes

"Whatever you can do, or dream you can – begin it. Boldness has genius, power and magic in it."

Johann Goethe

"A good objective of leadership is to help those who are doing poorly, to do well; and to help those who are doing well, to do even better."

Jim Rohn

"It's kind of fun to do the impossible."

Walt Disney

"You have to enable and empower people to make decisions independent of you. As I've learned, each person on a team is an extension of your leadership; if they feel empowered by you, they will magnify your power to lead."

Tom Ridge

"The challenge of leadership is to be Strong, but not rude.
Kind, but not weak.
Bold, but not bully.
Thoughtful, but not lazy.
Humble, but not timid.
Proud, but not arrogant.
Have humor, but without folly."

Jim Rohn

"No institution can possibly survive if it needs geniuses or supermen to manage it. It must be organized in such a way so as to be able to get along under the leadership composed of average human beings."

Peter Drucker

"The day the soldiers stop bringing you their problems, is the day you have stopped leading them. They have either lost confidence that you can help them, or concluded that you do not care. Either case is a failure of leadership."

Collin Powel

"Leaders must create passions. Love is the strongest of all passions - for it attacks simultaneously the head, the heart and the senses."

Lao Tzu

"Beaten paths are for beaten men."

Eric Johnston

"Failure is not a person – it is an event. A failure can be best described as a postponed success. The habit of persistence and perseverance is the habit of victory."

Herbert Kaufman

"The final test of a leader is that he leaves behind him in other men, the conviction and the will to carry on."

Walter Lippmann

Global Leadership Practices

Google

"Never settle for the best.
Great just isn't good enough. Google does not accept being the best as an endpoint, but a starting point. Through innovation and iteration, Google takes something that works well and improves upon it in unexpected ways."

Larry Page – founder, Google

Google...

Beyond Financial Returns

"Our goal is to develop services that significantly improve the lives of as many people as possible. In pursuing this goal, we may do things that we believe have a positive impact on the world, even if the near term financial returns are not obvious. For example, we make our services as widely available as we can by supporting over 90 languages and by providing most services for free."

Google...

Continuous Innovation – not instant perfection

- "We try a lot of innovative things, and many of them won't be successful. At first it can be hard to tell the difference. Many products I thought were initially so-so have become huge successes — our ads system, for instance, took quite a while and many improvements before its achievements became clear.
- An important part of our development process is our willingness to experiment publicly. Our teams are more productive once they get real users and feedback. We have learned that the best way to make something great is to actually launch it to the public."

Google...

Freedom to Employees

Google employees have "20 percent time" – effectively one day per week–in which they are free to pursue projects they are passionate about and think will benefit Google. The results of this creative effort already include products such as Google News, Google Suggest and Orkut – products which might otherwise have taken an entire start-up company to create and launch.

Google...

Exceptional People & Meaningful Work

"We believe we have created a work environment that attracts exceptional people. We know that people value meaning in their work; they want to be involved with things that are important and that are going to make a difference. That is what we let them do at Google. We give them autonomy by structuring projects around small teams".

Google...

70-20-10

Google spends 70% time in the core activities, 20% time is reserved for the adjacent activities and 10% of the organization's time is reserved for innovation.

Google...

Don't Be Evil.

The founders and Googlers (the employees, as they are called) believe strongly that in the long term, they will be better served—as shareholders and in all other ways—by a company that does good things for the world, even if they forgo some short term gains. This is an important aspect of Google's culture and is broadly shared by everyone in the company.

Daimler Chrysler...

Value Based Management

The main aim of value-based management is to ensure that Daimler Chrysler attains its **profit objectives,** boosts profitability across all business units and posts profitable growth in the interests of its customers, stockholders and employees.

Daimler Chrysler...

Management by Objectives

- In a multi-stage top-down process, the company's targets are broken down into profit targets for specific periods for each business unit.
- The targets are then translated into goals for the employees at the various plants and departments.
- These form the basis for the annual planning and binding goal agreement between management and employees. The employees then take direct responsibility for their work and for meeting their targets.

Daimler Chrysler...

Quality Leadership

- Within their respective fields, the business units are directly responsible for their operations. They are also responsible for ensuring that the agreed earnings targets are met.
- Value-based management aims to ensure sound operating results and a convincing style of leadership. Consequently, one measure of the quality of leadership is : **"how" targets are achieved?**

Daimler Chrysler...

Target Agreements

- Target agreements play a pivotal part in the annual leadership process. This management tool provides an effective means of attaining the strategic and operational targets of the company's individual business units. A year-end review of the degree to which targets have been achieved assure fair performance-based compensation.
- To achieve their objectives, the company follows **LEAD** (Leadership Evaluation And Development).

Daimler Chrysler...

LEAD Program

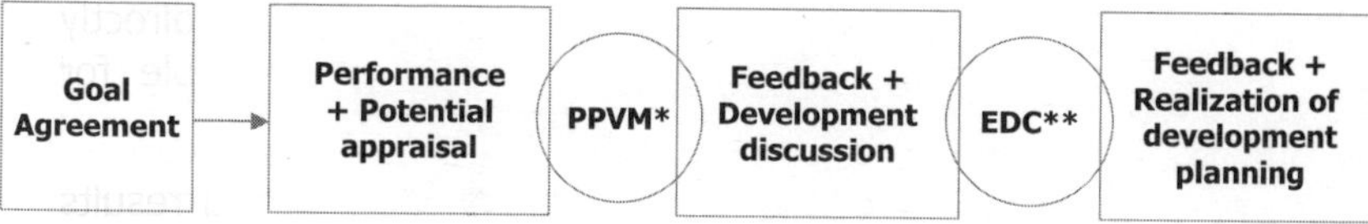

*** Performance and Potential Validation Meeting**
****Executive Development Conference**

INTEL Practices

INTEL...
Vision

"Advancing life through technology"

Today, Intel, the world's largest chip maker is also a leading manufacturer of computer, networking and communications products. Intel develops solutions that transform the way people live, work, communicate and play.

INTEL...
Customer Practices

- Listen and respond to customers, suppliers and stakeholders continuously.
- Clearly communicate mutual intentions and expectations.
- Deliver innovative and competitive products and services.
- Make it easy to work with us.
- Be vendor of choice.

INTEL...

Quality Practices

- Achieve the highest standards of excellence.
- Do the right things right.
- Continuously learn, develop and improve.
- Take pride in our work.

INTEL...

Discipline

- Conduct business with uncompromising integrity and professionalism.
- Ensure a safe, clean and injury-free workplace.
- Make and meet commitments.
- Properly plan, fund and staff projects.
- Pay attention to detail.

INTEL...

Innovation

- Foster innovation and creative thinking.
- Embrace change and challenge the status-quo.
- Listen to all ideas and viewpoints.
- Learn from our successes and mistakes.
- Encourage and reward informed risk taking.

INTEL...

Great Place to Work

- Be open and direct.
- Promote a challenging work environment that develops our diverse workforce.
- Work as a team with respect and trust for each other.
- Win and have fun.
- Recognize and reward accomplishments.
- Manage performance fairly and firmly.
- Be an asset to our communities worldwide.

INTEL...
Results

- Set challenging and competitive goals.
- Focus on output.
- Assume responsibility.
- Constructively confront and solve problems.
- Execute flawlessly.

Vision & Strategy

Leadership and Vision

Many definitions of leadership involve an element of 'Vision'. A vision is an **inspirational picture** of the future. Excellence in leadership requires reaching out to the employees through a vibrant vision statement, which offers:

- Clarity amidst confusion.
- Hope amidst despair.
- Unity of purpose amidst diversity of personal causes.

Organizational Vision

- An organizational vision offers a **compelling method** for forging employees into empowered, highly motivated team. It adds purpose to employee's lives and is the cornerstone of the strategic architecture of a truly successful organization.
- A good vision statement must be rational and creative, cerebral and passionate, **demanding yet friendly.**
- The following steps are involved in making an effective vision.

1. Preserve the Core

- The vision must preserve the **core competencies and values** of the organization, while stimulating progress towards the future. Without the core values, the vision will not be rooted in the organization. It will simply be a product of the imagination of its creators - putting it out of reach, both in operational and strategic terms.
- Merck's vision is built on its value of corporate social responsibility and science based innovation. Similarly Sony's vision rests on values of encouraging individual creativity and its determination to be a pioneer.

2. Identify Core Purpose

The next step after core values is to identify the core purpose of the organization. For instance, 3M declares that its purpose is to solve problems innovatively. Similarly, Nike announces that it wants to provide the experience and emotion of competition : Winning and crushing competitors.

3. Vision Must Originate from Employees

- It is extremely important to ensure that the vision comes directly from the employees. The organization must elicit ideas from employees on the characteristics of their dream organization.
- The vision of the organization must be shared by all the employees. It must be the starting point of a process that culminates in setting specific quantifiable objectives for every division or business unit, every section, every department and every employee.
- The core function of the organizational vision is to ignite the people into thinking beyond the company's existing capabilities and the present environment - and only a shared vision can achieve that.

Vision- Ingredients

- Appear as a simple, yet **vibrant.**
- Describe a **future** , credible and preferable to the present state.
- Act as a **bridge** between the present and a future optimum state.
- Appear desirable enough to **energize** followers.
- Convey to the followers at an **emotional or spiritual** level.

Presenting vision statements of global business leaders...

General Electric - Vision

- At GE, we believe some of the **world's most pressing challenges present an opportunity** to do what we do best: imagine and build innovative solutions that benefit our customers and society at large.
- As a global leader in energy, technology, manufacturing, and infrastructure, GE is uniquely suited to help solve environmental challenges profitably, today and for generations to come.
- Our customers want a more prosperous, cleaner future. By harnessing our most abundant renewable resource - the imagination of our people - we can create that future with them.
- We are taking a new approach to solving some of our customers' toughest environmental problems. We call it **ecomagination.**

Intel - Vision

- At Intel, we constantly push the boundaries of innovation in order to make people's lives more exciting, more fulfilling, and easier to manage. Our unwavering commitment to moving technology forward has transformed the world by leaps and bounds.
- We're a company that's always in motion, fueling an industry that never rests. We inspire our partners to develop innovative products and services, rally the industry to support new products, and drive industry standards. We do this so that we can collectively deliver better solutions with greater benefits more quickly.

General Motors - Vision

Our vision is to be the world leader in transportation products and related services. In order to achieve this vision, we recognize that many issues must be addressed and many goals attained. It is imperative that economic, environmental and social objectives be integrated into our daily business objectives and future planning activities so that we can become a more sustainable company.

Samsung - Vision

Recognizing that the 'digital revolution' is entering a new phase, Samsung Electronics has transformed it's operations by putting digital technology at the core. The company is committed to being a **market-driven solutions** provider and leader in digital convergence. With core competencies in semiconductors and CDMA technologies, Samsung Electronics creates digital solutions for homes, mobile users and offices that enable seamless communications, facilitate business transactions, access to the internet and offer digital entertainment.

Strategy

- The strategic approach must be an on going process and must concentrate on assuring a **good fit** between the environment and the organization.
- The strategic approach must take into account competitors, customers, external environment including technology, politics, economics and the social factors.
- The strategic approach has three processes:
  - Strategy formulation.
  - Strategy implementation.
  - Strategy evaluation.

Strategy Formulation

- Performing a situation analysis, conducting SWOT analysis to identify organization's strengths & weaknesses, competitor analysis, environmental analysis - both at micro and macro levels and key issues confronting the organization.
- Clarification of the organization's mission and various objectives in quantifiable terms.
- Formulation of a strategic plan, which stipulates the methodology of achieving the desired objectives.

Strategy Implementation

- Allocation of sufficient resources – Financial, personnel, technology support, time etc.
- Establishing a chain of command.
- Assigning responsibility of specific tasks.
- Managing the process. This includes monitoring results, comparing to benchmarks and best practices and evaluating the efficacy and efficiency of various processes.

Strategy Evaluation

- This requires the organizations to measure the effectiveness of the organizational strategy.
- Re-assess each strategy annually or quarterly to determine how it has been implemented.
- Determine whether the strategy has succeeded or needs replacement by a new strategy to meet changed circumstances, technology, competitors, economic environment, social and political developments.

Action Points

"I have been impressed with the urgency of doing. Knowing is not enough; we must apply. Being willing is not enough; we must do."

Leonardo-Da-Vinci

"I saw that leaders placed too much emphasis on what some call high-level strategy, on intellectualizing and philosophizing and not enough on implementation."

Larry Bossidy & Ram Charan / The Discipline of Getting Things Done

**"It gets back to planning versus acting:
We act from day one;
others plan how to plan - for months."**

Bloomberg

Creating Effective Collaboration

Historically, organizational design meant organizational structure. Today, it means the **alignment** of structure, management processes, information systems and people.

Conflicting Goals

The major challenge for the leader will be the **reconciliation of conflicting goals** like, thinking long-term while delivering short- term results and investing in innovation while maximizing the operational efficiency.

Creating Effective Collaboration

Whether it is various departments in the organizations, teams in departments or even individual in teams - there is a potential competition among various components and varying degrees of collaboration between them.

Creating effective collaboration within and between different groups is the most important challenge for the leader today.

Integrative Thinking

Rather than the charisma, leaders will be known for the processes they create. **Integrative thinking** - the ability to link internal processes and systems with the external world will be the most desirable leadership quality. Innovation will be at premium and will need to be guided by structured creative process.

Knowledge Management

Leaders will have to develop knowledge management systems within their organizations. Business processes will have to be re-defined around knowledge and not materials or capital. Leaders will have to create knowledge centres, which should be able to capture knowledge and disseminate it across the organization for use as a competitive weapon.

Action Points...

Leaders establish unity of purpose and direction of the organization. They should create and maintain the internal environment in which people can become fully involved in achieving the organization's objectives. This requires the following steps :

- Establish long term vision and strategy.
- Enlist others in a common vision by appealing to their values, interests, hopes and dreams.

Action Points...

- Search for **challenging opportunities** to change, grow, innovate and improve.
- Experiment, take risk and learn from mistakes.
- Foster collaboration by promoting co-operative goals and building trust.

Action Points...

- Strengthen others by sharing information & power.
- Set an example by behaving in the ways that is consistent with the stated values.
- Plan small wins. This will result in promoting consistent progress and build commitment & enthusiasm.
- Recognize individual contributions to the success of every project.

Action Points...

- Invest in long term research and innovation.
- Foster and promote 'Excellence work-culture' where talent can bloom and the individual brilliance is given a free hand.
- Create entrepreneurial islands, which provide job challenge and meaningful opportunities to employees in a **win-win manner**.
- Continuously steer the organization and support people for meeting the expectations of the customers, stakeholders and society.

Delivering Performance

Thus the new age leaders will be known:

- Less for what they say and more for what they deliver.
- Less by the goals they set and more by the mindsets they build.
- Less by what they control and more by what they innovate.

Decoding LEADERSHIP

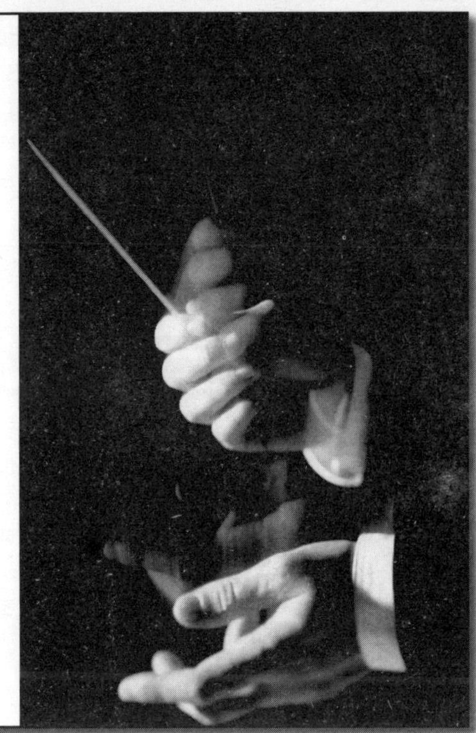

LEADERSHIP

Learning

Both - organizational learning and personal learning are extremely important for achieving the highest standards of excellence. Learning can result in enhancing value to customers, developing new opportunities and overall business performance.

LEADERSHIP

Execution

Execution is the most important aspect of leadership, failing which all the plans and projects remain simply on papers. Leadership must act fast and expect others to act fast as well.

LEADERSHIP

Agility

Success in today's ever changing, globally competitive environment demands 'AGILITY' – a capacity for rapid change and flexibility. Organizations face ever-shorter cycles for new products & services and prompt responsiveness to changing dynamics keeps the organization miles ahead of the competition.

LEADERSHIP

Daring

Leaders must be daring and courageous.

Different

Leaders must relentlessly follow the policy of being different. They must have different products, different business models, different work-style and different strategies to stay ahead and sustain the competitive advantages.

LEADERSHIP

Excellence always

Nothing less than 'EXCELLENCE' should be provided to the customers. Similarly nothing less than 'excellent' should be expected from the work force and suppliers.

LEADERSHIP

Risk taking

Leaders must have the ability of taking well informed and calculated risks.

LEADERSHIP

Soft skills

Leaders must have 'soft skills' to get the best out of people. They must develop passionate people and lead by using the emotional quotient. They must generate lot of excitement and enthusiasm. They must truly inspire people and become their role models. They must genuinely share their joys and sorrows.

LEADERSHIP

Hard skills

Leaders must possess 'hard skills' as well. They must set the targets and demand excellent performance. They must act with authority when the situation demands. They must hold others accountable for the desired results. They must balance the soft and hard skills very well to derive the desired results.

LEADERSHIP

Innovation

Innovation should be the top most priority of a leader for succeeding in the 21st century. Innovation differentiates between the leaders and the followers. Leaders must focus on developing new products and services. They must encourage lot of creativity and out-of-the-box thinking. They must also encourage people to experiment, fail, but succeed finally.

LEADERSHIP

Privilege

Leadership is a great privilege to better the lives of others.

Performance

Great leadership is – 'Great performance delivered.' Performance is the ultimate measure of the effectiveness of leadership. Leaders must deliver the desired results for the customers, people, stake-holders and the society at large.

3

People

Excellence Culture

"People want to be part of something **larger** than themselves. They want to be part of something they're really proud of, that they'll fight for, sacrifice for, trust."

Howard Schultz, Starbucks

"The best thing a leader can do for a great group is to allow its members to discover their **greatness**."

Warren Bennis and Patricia Ward Biederman - 'Organizing Genius'

"Never doubt that a small group of committed people can change the world. Indeed it is the **only thing** that ever has."

Margaret Mead

"To live is the rarest thing in the world. Most people exist, that is all."

Oscar Wilde

"Tell me, what is it you plan to do with your one wild and precious life?"

Mary Oliver

What is your personal benchmark?

The secret of 'Excellence' is contained in one word – 'Passion'. If you are passionate about your work, you will always enjoy it. If you enjoy what you do, you will EXCEL.

Involvement of People

People at all levels are the essence of an organization and their full involvement enables their abilities to be used for the organization's benefit. This requires the following steps:

- Employees must be treated with dignity and respect.
- They must be trained to build competence where required.
- Each employee must know what exactly is required to be done and where possible must be able to assess the quality of his work.
- Fear must be totally removed from the organization and employees must be encouraged to bring out problems in the system.

Involvement of People...

- Empower employees to take appropriate action in their area of work for improvement.
- In case of a mistake, examine the system rather than the man to prevent its recurrence.
- Assess employee satisfaction level and take appropriate measures to improve their morale so that they take pride in belonging to the company.

Excellence Culture

Since people are the **most important resources** for any organization, lot of efforts must be focused on developing the excellence or high-performance work culture.

Culture Has to Be Gradually Built

An organization's culture consists of **values, norms and practices** of its people. The culture of the organization can be best defined by observing and describing the behaviours of the people. Culture can only be changed, by changing the **organizational behaviours.**

Building the Excellence Culture

Quality results	Recognition & rewards
Quality action	Process ownership
Commitment & Integrity	Continuous improvement
Internal and external customer focus	Quality work environment
Organization loyalty to employees	Employee loyalty to organization
Top down leadership	Vision, Mission & Quality policy

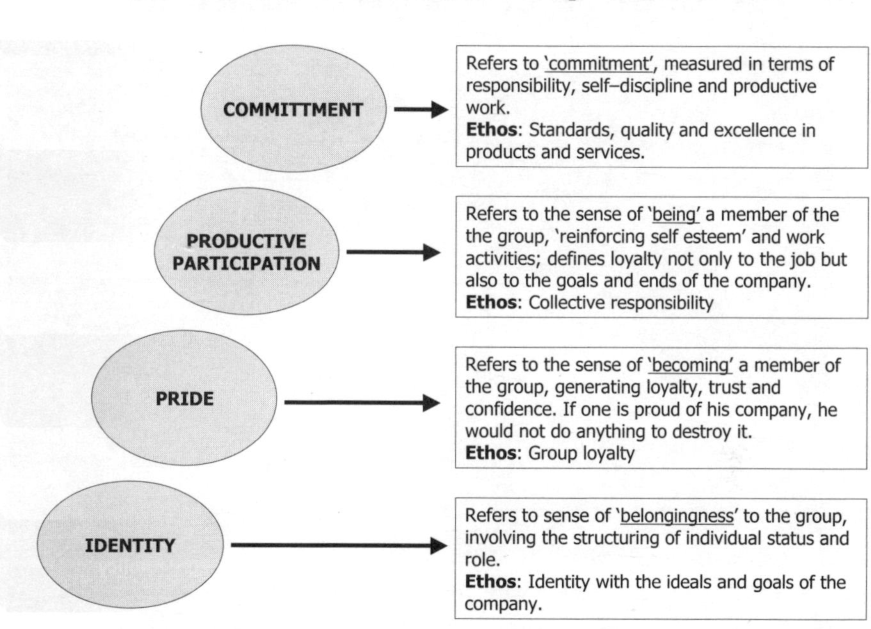

Changing to Excellence Culture

A. Change in people's attitude.

B. Change in management's attitude.

A. Change in People's Attitude

People's Behaviours

People must strive for **'Excellence'** in whatever they do. They must do exceptional, outstanding and extra-ordinary work in their respective areas.

They must develop a **positive attitude** for achieving excellence.

Developing a Positive Attitude

While considerable attention has been given to the technical side of 'Quality', there is an increasing need for the importance of the **human side to total quality** for developing the excellence culture.

True Assets

The greatest contribution to the organization is made by the people. People with right attitude and intellectual capital are the true assets of any organization in the knowledge driven economies.

Winning Instinct

In its original Japanese context, 'Total Quality' refers not only to the quality of management, which ultimately produces quality goods and services, but to the quality of human behavior, skills, commitment and the **winning instinct** necessary to accomplish the business objectives.

Beauty to the World

This not only makes good business sense, it also reflects a deeper yearning of the human spirit to be of service, to build loving, caring relationships, to affirm our inter-dependence and to bring **value, beauty & benefit into the world**.

Spirit of Quality

If we are to take **'Total Quality'** to heart, we too must come to look at our own lives in a more multidimensional, inter-related and holistic manner. Taking the theme of 'Total Quality' personally, has the potential to tap us into the flow of **life giving forces**, which are ultimately most rewarding and productive.

Elements of POSITIVE ATTITUDE

PASSION

PERSEVERANCE

ASPIRATIONS

DETERMINATION

HARD WORK

COMMITMENT

ENTHUSIASM

FIGHTING SPIRIT

FOCUS

STRONG DESIRE TO WIN

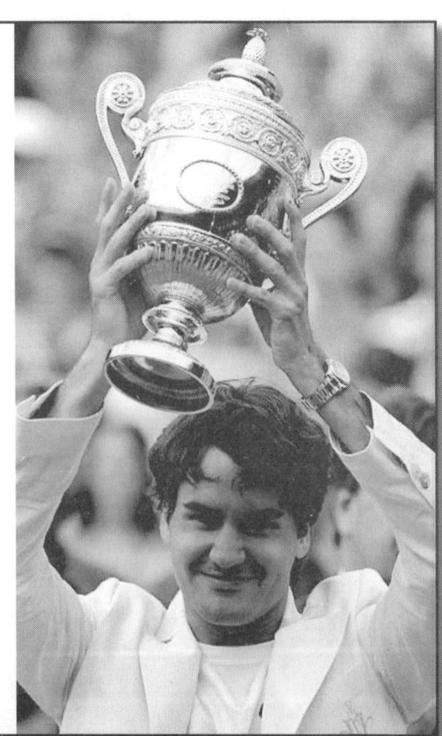

Do You Have a Positive Attitude?

Take an attitude test at the end of this section.

B. Change in Management's Attitude

This requires the management's focus on the following 3 fronts:

1. **Employee Motivation**
2. **Employee Recognition**
3. **Employee Retention**

1. Employee Motivation

Define Outcome

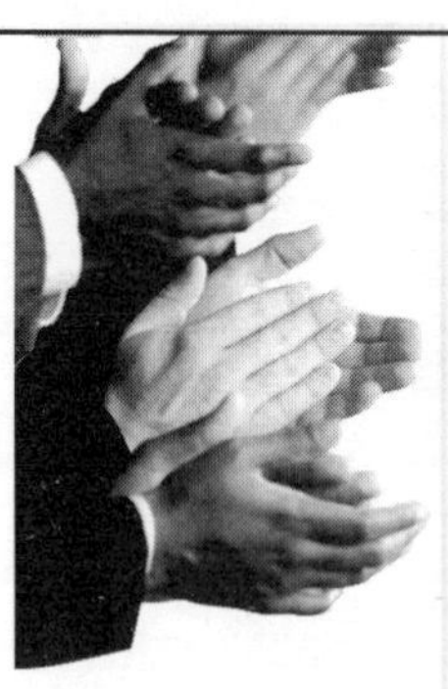

Define the **outcome** you want from the managers and insist that they find their own way there. This practice encourages creativity and makes people empowered enough to find their ways for achieving their goals.

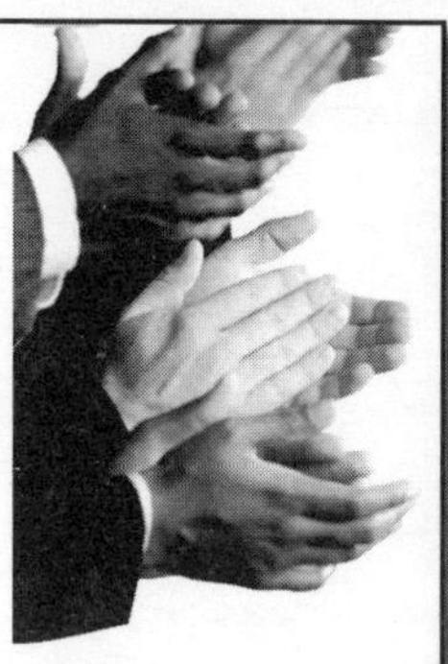

Identify Strengths

Identify **strengths of the employees** and make efforts to develop and use their strengths by assigning suitable jobs to them. The best way to motivate a person is to offer him the job which he / she likes the most.

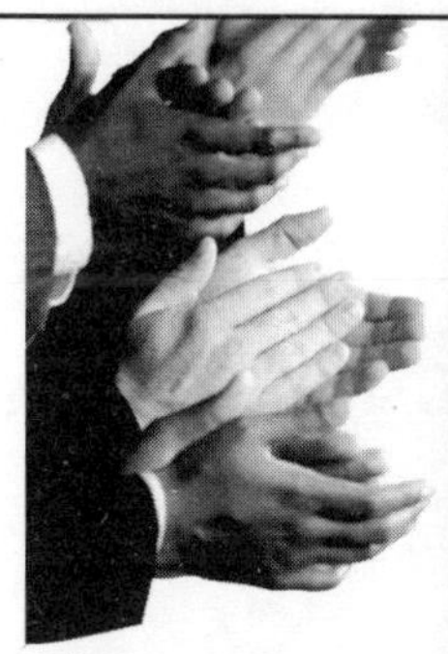

Share Joys

The seniors must genuinely **share the joys and sorrows of the individuals.** Treat every employee as a distinctive individual. Every individual is a unique bundle of needs, insecurities, ambitions, spirit and **genius**.

This must be translated into specific action in managing every individual's growth, training, rewards etc. In majority of cases the employees do not leave the organizations - they leave their seniors and supervisors.

Align Organizational Mission

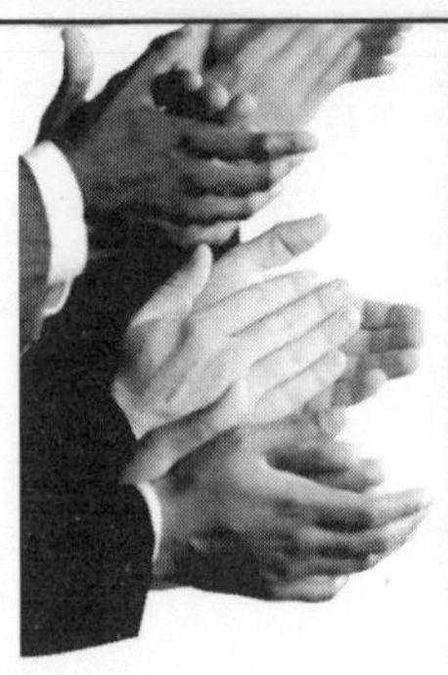

- To motivate a person to give his best to the organization, demonstrate to him, how his excellent contribution can make a significant difference to the overall performance of the organization. Their opinions must be considered during the decision making process.
- Assist the employees in translating organization's mission into personal mission.

Encourage Creativity

- Get the teams to initiate the continuous improvement process and recognize their achievements. This practice generates a lot of enthusiasm and excitement eventually resulting in commitment to work excellence. Encourage team based rewards rather than individual rewards.
- Encourage lot of creativity at work place. Give freedom to perform and nurture the passion of people. Allow people to experiment with new ideas and give them a free hand to perform.

Transparency

Create a work culture that is transparent, open to new ideas and promotes lot of creativity and innovation.

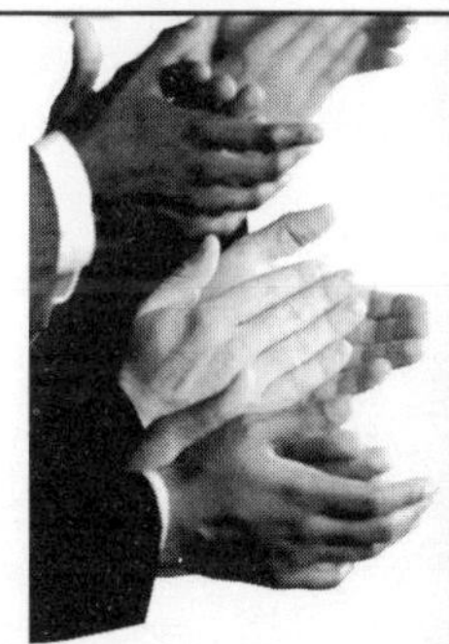

Create Great Work Places

It must be remembered that good pay and perks can always be improved by your competitors - it is only the great working environment, which can not be duplicated and therefore, will make a significant difference to the success of an organization.

2. Employee Recognition

Employee Recognition

- The whole competitive society that we live in, is driven by people striving to be **recognized.** Prioritize employee recognition and you can ensure a high-performance organizational climate.
- People who feel appreciated are more positive about themselves and their ability to contribute. People with positive self-esteem are potentially your best employees.
- When you recognize people effectively, you reinforce the actions and behaviors that must be repeated quite often in the interest of the organization.

Objectives of a Recognition Process

A good recognition process has the following major objectives:

- To provide recognition to employees, who make unusual contributions to the organization.
- To show organization's appreciation for superior performance.
- To leverage maximum benefits from the recognition process by effective communication.

Ingredients of a Recognition Process

- To provide many ways to recognize employees for their efforts and stimulate management creativity in the recognition process.
- To improve the employee morale through proper recognition.
- To reinforce behavioral patterns.

Types of Recognition

1. **Financial compensation**
2. **Monetary rewards**
3. **Individual public recognition**
4. **Group public recognition**

Categories of Exceptional Contribution

The following categories of exceptional contributions should never go un-noticed & must be recognised for stimulating continuous improvement:

- Activity that results in significant savings & increased income.
- Acts where a person has gone out of the way to serve the customer.
- Creative problem solving.
- Innovation.

3. Employee Retention

Attracting and Retaining People

Attracting, managing and **nurturing talent** are extremely important factors for achieving sustained business growth. This calls for pro-active measures on three fronts.

Attracting and Retaining People

- Organizations will have to create an ambience where talent can bloom.
- They have to put in place systems that will help unleash the potential of their employees.
- They have to build a reward and recognition mechanism that provides value for people.

Exciting Opportunities

The dynamic market environment will give rise to lot many entrepreneurial opportunities, which will take away talent from even the best organizations. Thus the take home pay cheque will seize to be a major motivator.

Sense of Fun

Exciting opportunities and meaningful work with a sense of fun will be the preferred choice for the employees.

Entrepreneurial Islands

Organizations will have to create **small entrepreneurial islands,** where they can house their best talents to pursue experiments, innovate, develop cutting edge products, dream up new and better ways of doing business to create value in an **unrestricted manner.**

Secrets of Success

"Always bear in mind that your own resolution to success is more important than any other one thing."

Abraham Lincoln

Success Foundation Stones

"The wisdom of preparation.
The strength of courage.
The worth of honesty.
The privilege of working.
The discipline of struggle.
The satisfaction of serving.
The buoyancy of enthusiasm.
The advantage of initiative.
The fruitfulness of perseverance.
The virtue of patience.
The joy of winning."

Rollo C. Hester

"Success – the most priceless of human treasures – is available to all among us, without exception, to those who make 'good' things happen in the world around them."

Joe Klock

"If there is one great secret of success in life, it lies in the ability to put yourself in other person's place and to see things from his point of view – as well as your own."

Henry Ford

"Take a chance!
All life is a chance.
The man who goes farthest is generally the one who is willing to do and dare."

Dale Carnegie

"The only advice I can give to the person eager to have success – is to do whatever turns you on. If you are not doing something that's got you all wrapped up, you just can't do it well."

Malcolm Forbes

"Do not go where the path may lead, go instead where there is no path and leave a trail."

Ralph Waldo Emerson

"Success is connected with action, successful people keep moving. They make mistakes, but they don't quit. They never ever give up."

Conrad Hilton

"Put your heart, mind, intellect and soul even to your smallest acts. This is the secret of success."

Swami Sivananda

"Many of life's failures are people who did not realize how close they were to success when they gave up."

Thomas Edison

Attitude Test

Rank the following questions on 1 to 5 scale to know your Attitude score:
(1 is the lowest score and 5 is the highest score)

		Score
1	I am an energetic person.	
2	I have varied interests in life.	
3	I keep myself updated with current affairs.	
4	I am creative and innovative in resolving problems.	
5	I never ever give up.	
6	I always look at brighter side of things.	
7	I love to accept challenges and win over them.	
8	I am always happy.	
9	I create a good balance in my work and personal life.	
10	I like to network with people.	
11	I understand that every problem is also a big opportunity.	
12	I am always willing to help people, not always for money.	
13	I encourage others.	
14	I am self - motivated.	
15	I realize that 'today is the greatest day of my life'.	
16	I love to experiment new ideas.	
17	I work hard, really hard.	
18	I am proactive and act really fast.	
19	I don't allow a day to pass by without making some improvement.	
20	I think big, very very big.	
	Total	

Analyze your score:

0-40 **You need to seriously work on the attitude.**

41-60 **Average, lot of room for improvement.**

61-80 **Good, you can do better.**

81-100 **Great. You are a winner. Keep it up.**

4

Customers

Customer Driven Excellence

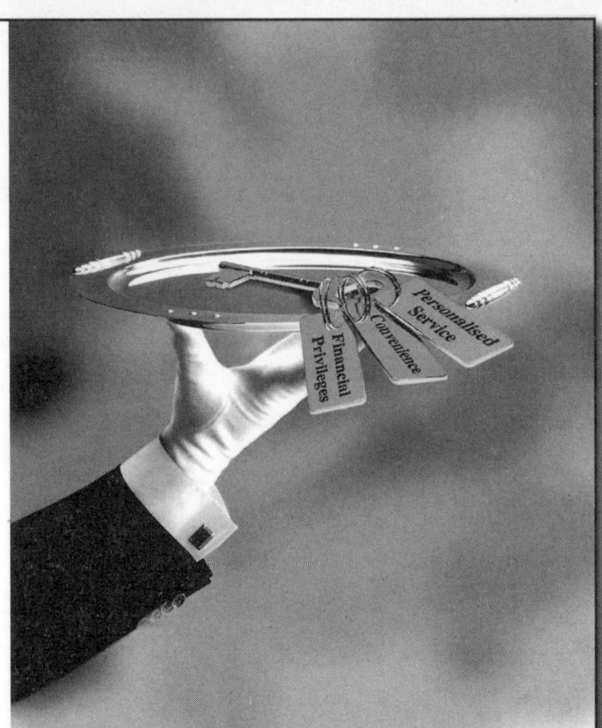

"When the customer comes first, the customer will last."

Robert Half

"Your most unhappy customers are your greatest source of learning."

Bill Gates in Business@ Speed of Thought

"There is only one boss - the customer. He can fire everybody in the company from the chairman to managers, simply by spending his money somewhere else."

Sam Walton

Invert the Organization to Become Customer Focused

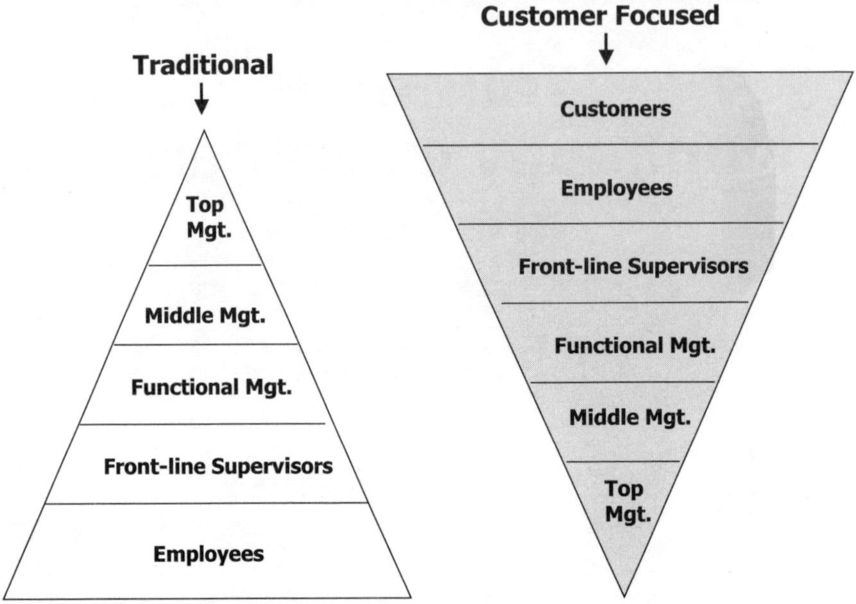

Customer Feedback & Improvement

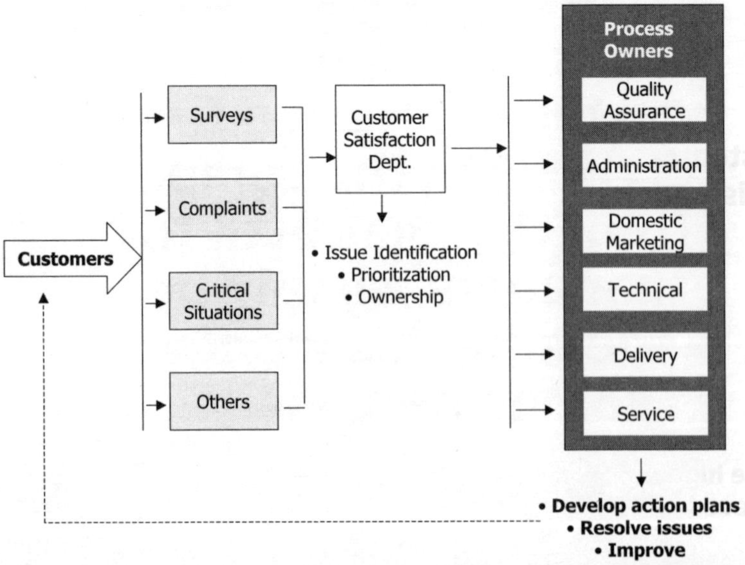

Customer Satisfaction

$$\text{Customer Satisfaction} = \frac{\text{Product quality / values}}{\text{Price the customer pays}}$$

$$\text{Customer Satisfaction} = \frac{\text{Product quality / values}}{\text{Price the customer pays}}$$

The higher degrees of customer satisfaction levels can be achieved either by increasing the product quality or reducing the price.

Components of Product Value

- Performance
- Reliability
- Durability
- Serviceability
- Aesthetics
- Perceived quality

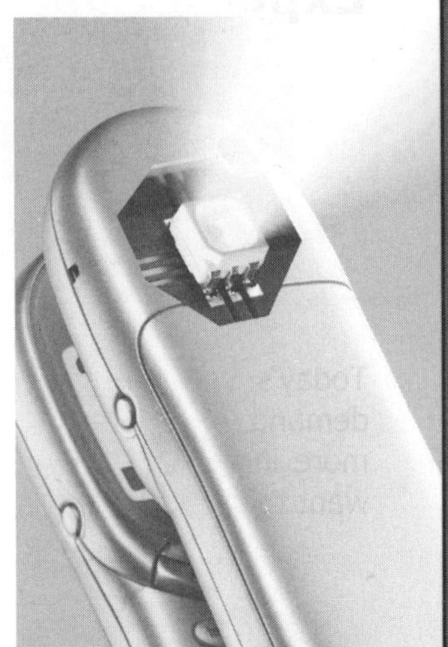

Components of Service Value

- Security
- Reliability
- Accessibility
- Timeliness
- Responsiveness
- Empathy
- Assurance

Customer Expectations

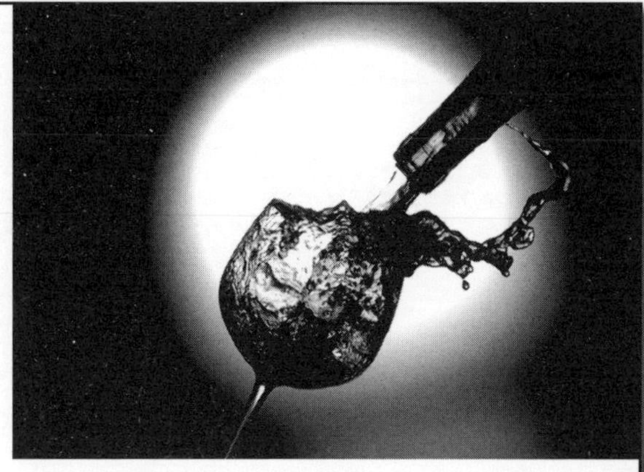

Today's customers are demanding **more than ever before.** They demand more quality, more service, more choice and most importantly, more innovation in times to come. For getting all these benefits, they want to spend less time, efforts and money.

More for Less

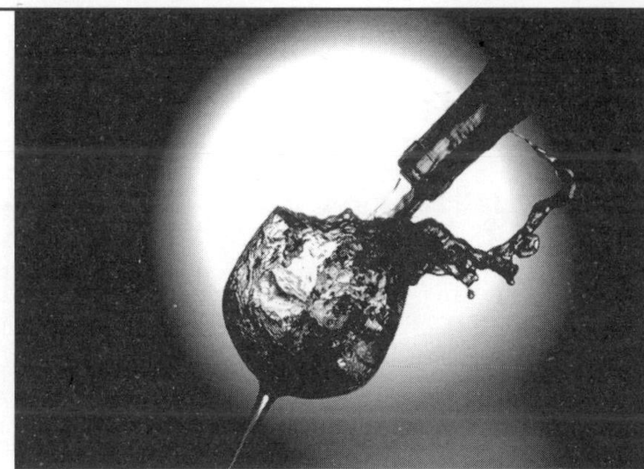

Customer's directives and expectations to the market place are loud and clear – "**Give us more for less"** and fulfillment of this expectation alone can create customer delight.

No Choice

The organizations do not have the choice of either **'quality' or 'price'** as their differentiators any more. They will have to provide both quality and price advantages to the customers to remain globally competitive.

'More for Less'

Well captured in Honda's policy

"Maintaining an international viewpoint, we are dedicated to supplying products of the **highest efficiency** yet at a **reasonable price** for worldwide customer satisfaction."

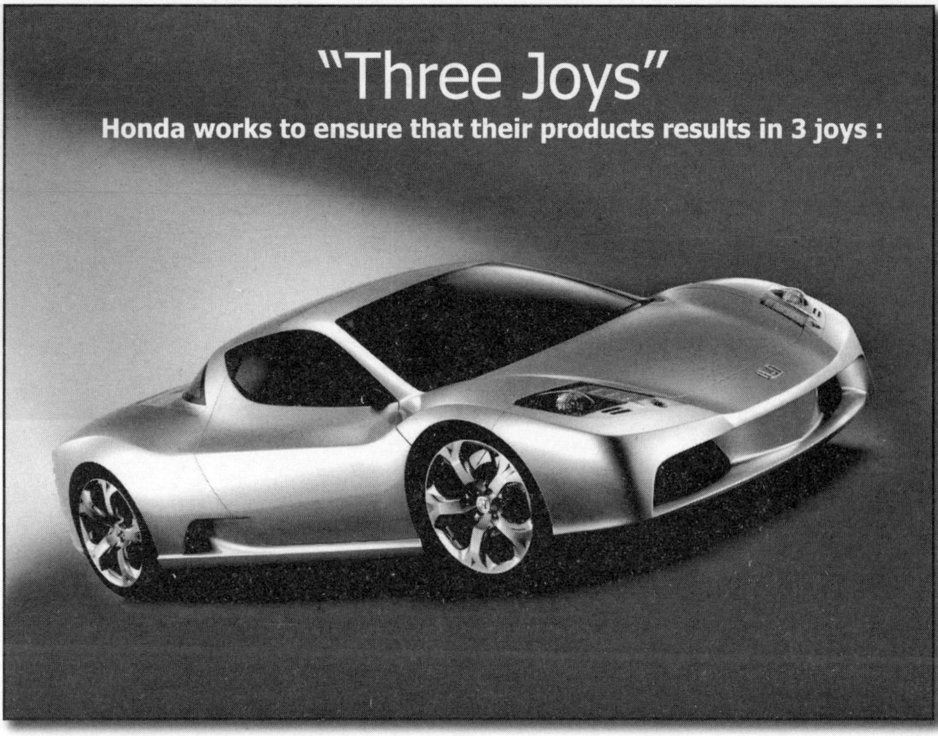

"Three Joys"

Honda works to ensure that their products results in 3 joys :

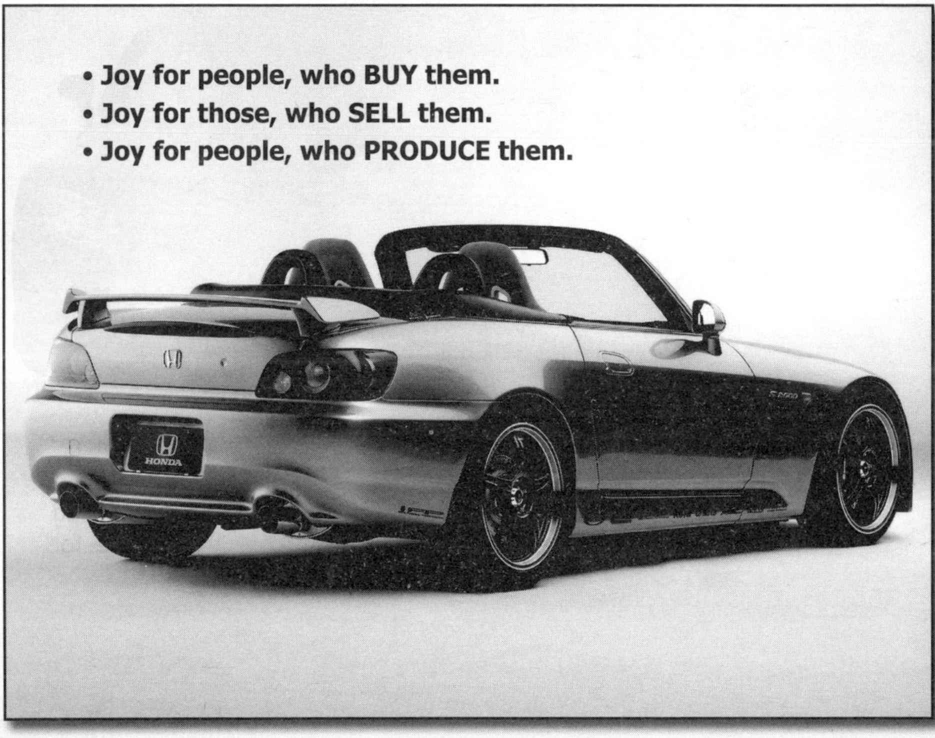

- **Joy for people, who BUY them.**
- **Joy for those, who SELL them.**
- **Joy for people, who PRODUCE them.**

Global Leaders Provide 'More for Less'

- Hewlett Packard: **MORE** in one - Fax, copier, scanner and printer.
- Intel Centrino Duo: Do **MORE**.
- IBM**: MORE** performance.
- Tata Indica: **MORE** car per car.
- Airtel: Talk **MORE** for less.
- ICICI: The card that rewards you **MORE**.
- Indian Oil: **MORE** miles.
- Business Today: **MORE** influential.
- Siemens: **MORE** productivity.
- Toyota Innova: **MORE** togetherness.

From 'Customer Satisfaction' to 'Customer Success'

The term 'MORE for LESS' is equated with customer's desire to become **more successful**. Organizations moving towards business excellence must understand this aspect of customer's mind-set very clearly and develop products and services, which ultimately make their customers more successful. They must make products which makes their customers more productive, competitive, healthier, smarter, comfortable and faster.

Linking with Success Factors

Marketing excellence requires the organizations to link their products & services with the ultimate success factors of their customers.

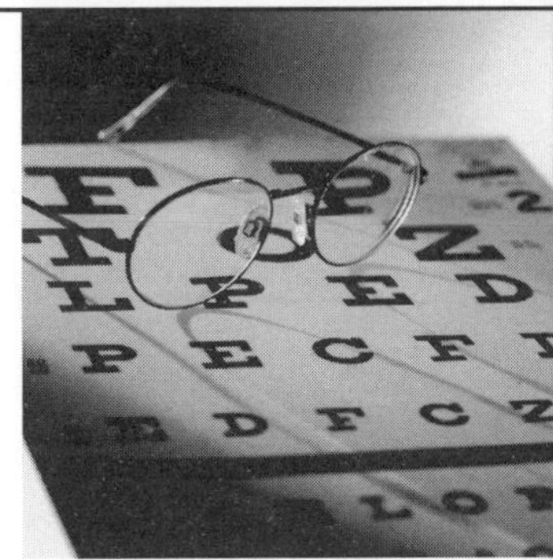

Advertisement by an Eye Care Company

"You are worried about your two eyes, we are more concerned about hundreds of employees working under you."

Success factors

- More productive
- Business performance

Advertisement by Packing and Forwarding Company

We call our trucks 'Locker on wheels'

<u>Success factor</u>

More secure

Advertisement by Projector Company

"Our projectors enable in enhancement of teacher's performance and student's comprehension levels."

<u>Success factor</u>

More productivity of teachers and students.

Customer Loyalty

"Customer satisfaction is worthless, customer loyalty is priceless." - *Book by Jeffrey Gitomer*

Customer loyalty is the feeling of **attachment and affection** for company's products, services or people. Organization's products must have the competitive advantages for achieving higher degrees of customer loyalty.

Advantages of Loyal Customers

The company's loyal customers are also its most profitable customers. With each additional year of relationship, the customers become less costly to serve. They become the true business ambassadors, because they buy more and bring in more customers through referrals & word of mouth.

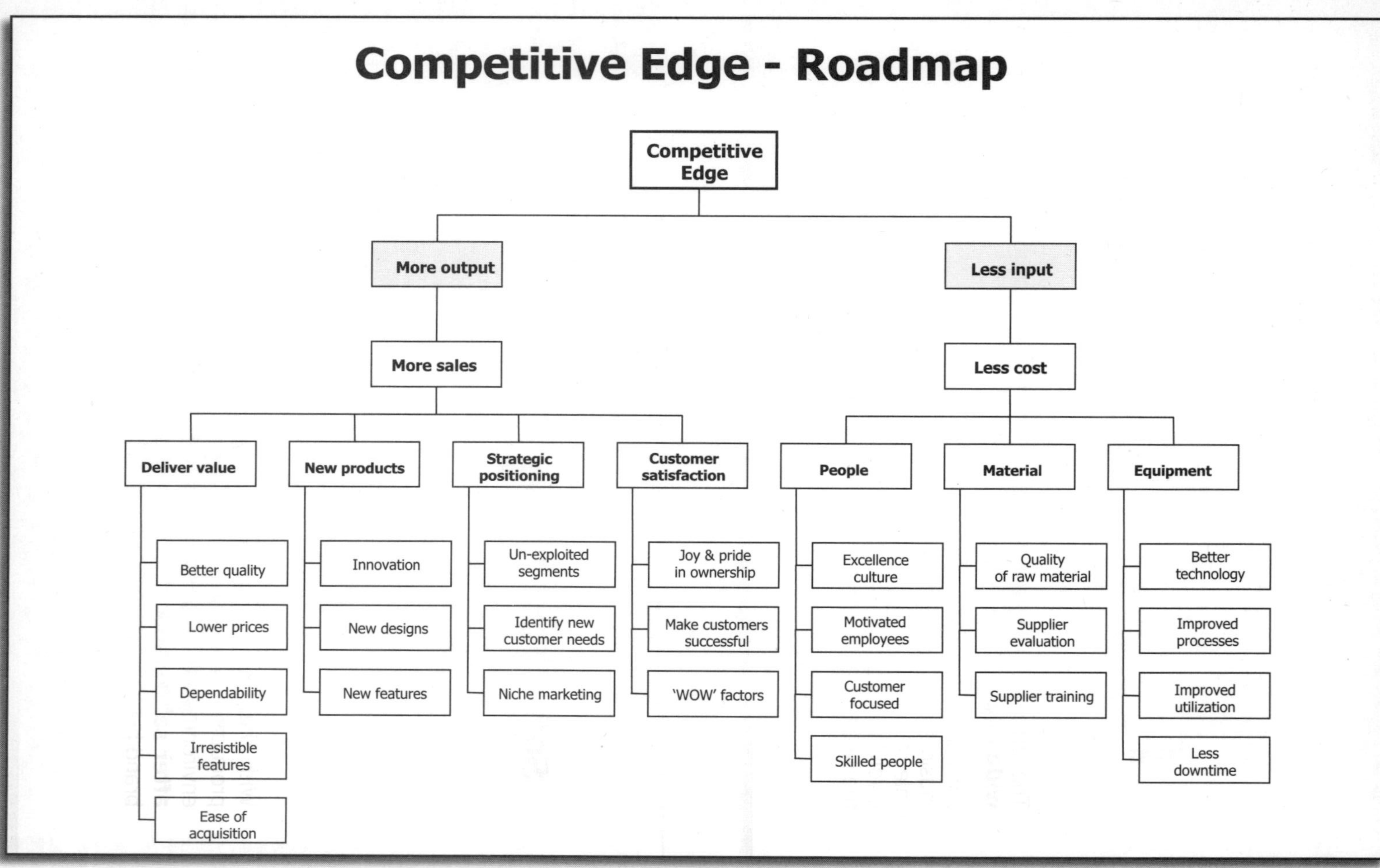
Competitive Edge - Roadmap
Competitive Edge
More output
Less input
More sales
Less cost
Deliver value
New products
Strategic positioning
Customer satisfaction
People
Material
Equipment
Better quality
Lower prices
Dependability
Irresistible features
Ease of acquisition
Innovation
New designs
New features
Un-exploited segments
Identify new customer needs
Niche marketing
Joy & pride in ownership
Make customers successful
'WOW' factors
Excellence culture
Motivated employees
Customer focused
Skilled people
Quality of raw material
Supplier evaluation
Supplier training
Better technology
Improved processes
Improved utilization
Less downtime

Wide Range of Products

The organizations must take long term perspective and **develop a wide range of value added products for their customers.**

For example, a good experience with a T.V can result in the sale of a music system, the satisfaction with the music system can result in the sale of a camera and so on. The organization must evolve a strategy of involving their customers in the chain of products – each one leading to the sale of another.

Soft Part of Quality

With the advancement of production technology, the differences in products of various brands will eventually diminish. In this environment it is the soft part of quality, i.e **method of delivery and after sales service,** which will become the differentiating factor in brand building and earning customer loyalty.

Reasons for Shift in Customer Loyalty

- Dissatisfaction from products / services / people.
- Entry of new products / competitors.
- Lost customer contacts.
- Reduction in brand dominance.
- Company image / poor financial results.

Components of Customer Loyalty

- **Quality:** Zero defects.
- **Uniformity:** Zero variation.
- **Reliability:** Zero field failures.
- **Dependability:** Towards lifetime guarantee.
- **Maintainability:** Towards accurate, fast & low cost of repairs.
- **Diagnostics:** Towards customer self-diagnostic.
- **Availability:** Towards 100% up-time.
- **Technical performance:** State-of-the-art technology.
- **Ergonomics:** Styling / Color / Ease of operation / User-friendliness.
- **Core features:** Expected by the customer.
- **Delight Features:** Unexpected features that thrill customers.

Components of Customer Loyalty...

- **Safety:** Product usage and user product liability prevention.
- **Design:** State-of-the-art / Amazing / 'WOW'.
- **Service before sales:** Behaviour / Co-operation / Communication.
- **Service after sales:** Sustained contact and interest after sales.
- **Delivery:** Short cycle-time.
- **Price:** Below competition.
- **Resale value:** High percentage of purchase price.
- **Reputation:** Image / Perceived quality.

"Marketing is not the art of finding clever ways to dispose off what you make. It is the art of creating Genuine Customer Value."

Philip Kotler

"The aim of marketing is to know and understand the customer so well that the product or service fits him and sells itself. The ultimate goal of marketing is to make sales superfluous, unimportant and non-essential."

Peter Drucker

"In marketing, I've seen only one strategy that can't miss - and that is to market to your best customers first, your best prospects second and the rest of the world last."

John Romero

"The customer you lose holds the information you need to succeed."

Frederick F.Reichheld

"A real salesman does not attempt to sell his prospect but instead directs his efforts towards putting the prospect in a frame of mind so that he will be moved to action by a given set of facts."

Roy Howard

"Once you have sold to a customer, make sure he is satisfied with your goods. Stay with him until the goods are used up or worn out. Your product may be of such long life that you will never sell him again, but he will sell you and your product to his friends."

William Feather

A good salesman must understand the products and services of the prospective customers, their business objectives, their customers, their competition and most importantly their problems and concerns. He must then skillfully try and make a 'good fit' between his product and the prospective customer's business objectives.

"Here's a pointer culled from the careers of men who have attained notable success: Don't sit in your office during the hours prospects can be seen. Do your office work before or after the hours during which possible customers can be reached. This may mean adding an hour or two quite often to your day's work; but in times like this particularly, the securing of a satisfactory amount of business through the expenditure of an extra hour or two a day is not an unreasonable price to pay."

B.C.Forbes

Quality Function Deployment (QFD)

Quality Function Deployment (QFD)

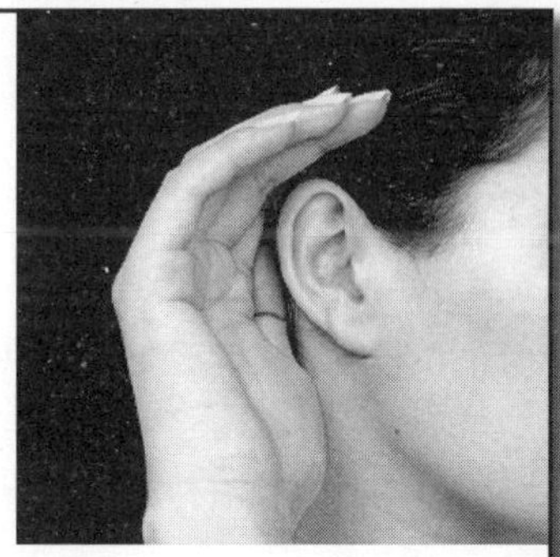

QFD is a scientific technique for translating the voice of the customer into development of new products and services. It is a complete **product planning process** as opposed to problem solving and analysis. The technique was invented by Akashi Fukuhara of Japan and first applied with very good results at Toyota.

Key Components of QFD Matrix

<table>
<tr><td></td><td>2.
Technical Requirements</td><td></td></tr>
<tr><td>1.
Customer Requirements</td><td>4.
Relating Customer Requirements to Technical Requirements</td><td>3.
Customer Competitive Assessment</td></tr>
<tr><td colspan="2">5.
Competitive Technical Assessment</td><td></td></tr>
<tr><td colspan="2">6.
Operational Goals</td><td></td></tr>
</table>

Step 1

List Customer Requirements and Rank

Customer Requirements	Importance on 10 point scale
Very Important	
Moderately Important	
Slightly Important	

Step 2
List Technical Requirements to Meet Customer Requirements

Step 3
Compare Product with the Nearest Competitor

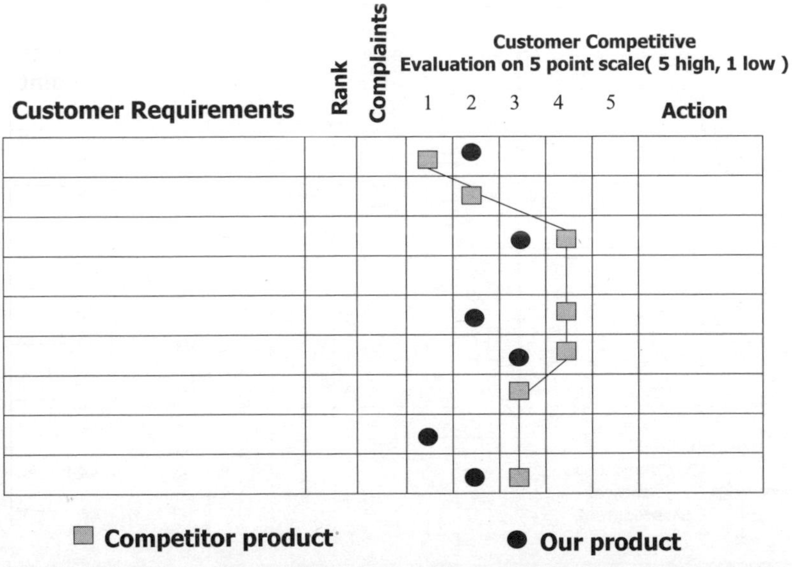

Customer Requirements | Rank | Complaints | Customer Competitive Evaluation on 5 point scale(5 high, 1 low) 1 2 3 4 5 | Action

■ Competitor product ● Our product

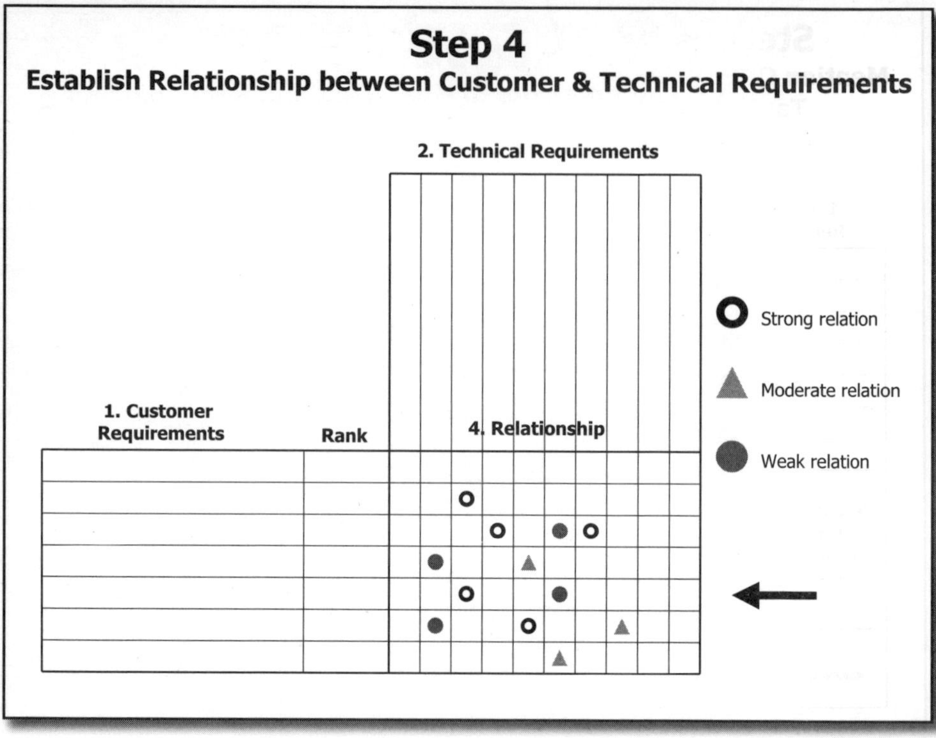

Step 4
Establish Relationship between Customer & Technical Requirements

2. Technical Requirements

1. Customer Requirements

Rank

4. Relationship

Strong relation

Moderate relation

Weak relation

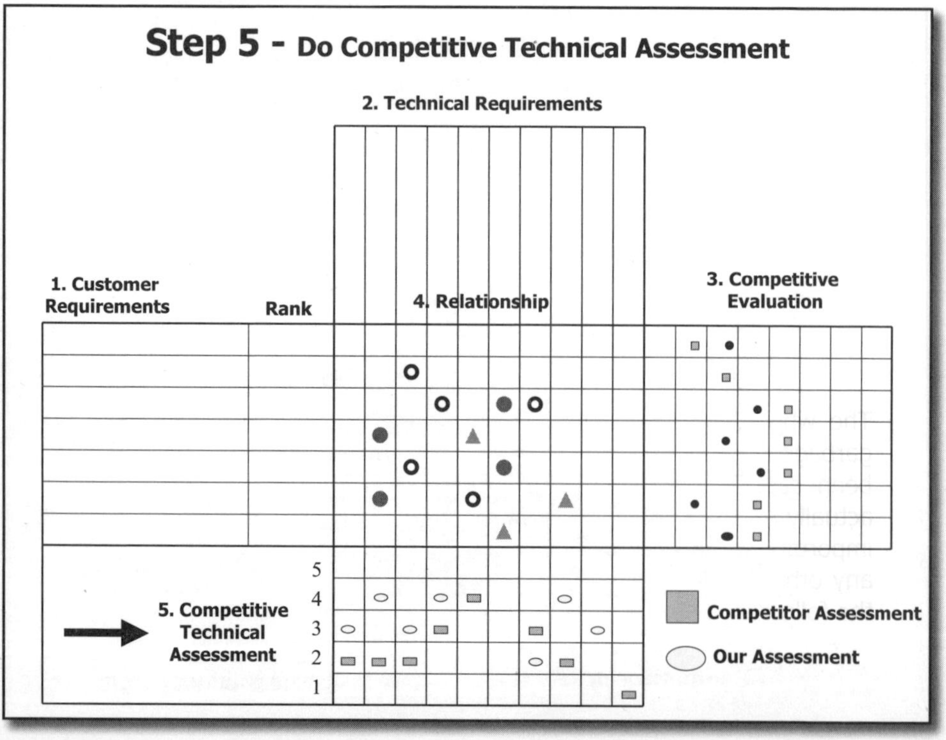

Step 5 - Do Competitive Technical Assessment

2. Technical Requirements

1. Customer Requirements

Rank

4. Relationship

3. Competitive Evaluation

5. Competitive Technical Assessment

5
4
3
2
1

Competitor Assessment

Our Assessment

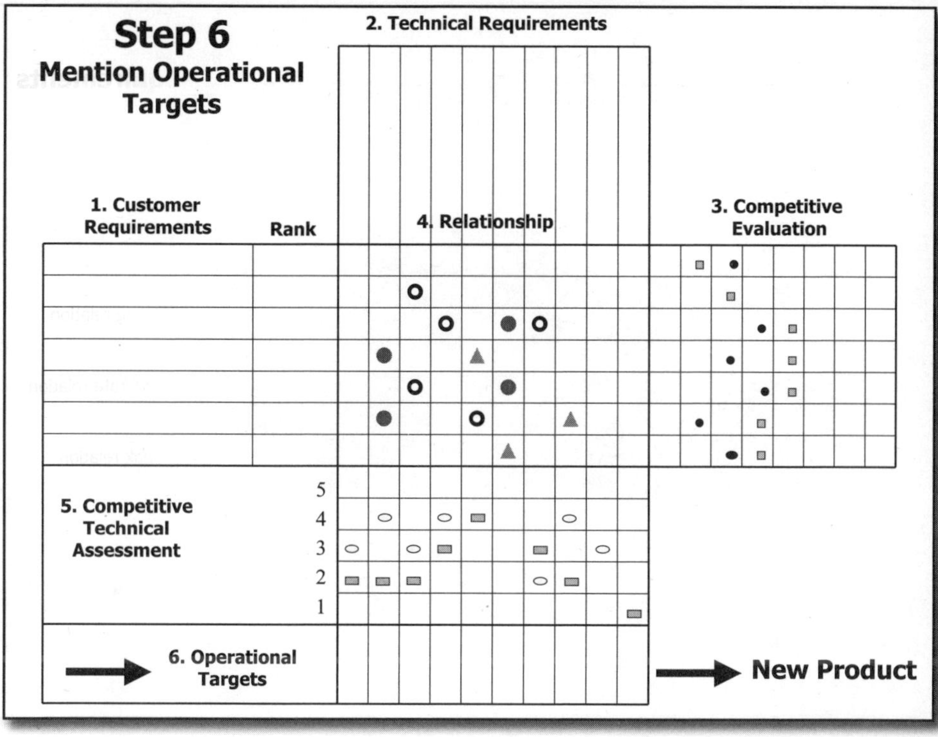

Step 6
Mention Operational Targets

2. Technical Requirements

1. Customer Requirements

Rank

4. Relationship

3. Competitive Evaluation

5. Competitive Technical Assessment

5
4
3
2
1

6. Operational Targets

New Product

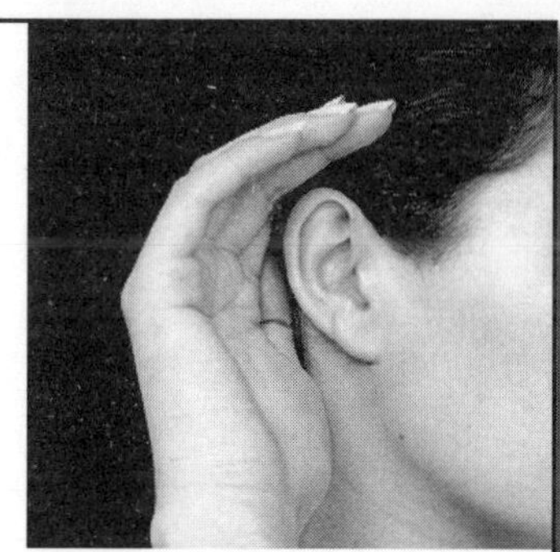

Customer's Voice

The whole process of the QFD can be linked to **GIGO** (Garbage in garbage out). This is because, if the voice of the customer has not been captured properly, the final product will also not be the one actually desired by the market place. It is, therefore, extremely important to capture the correct voice of the customer before taking any other step in the QFD planning process. This can be explained by the following example.

New Car Development

New Car Development

A product development team wants to determine the requirements of the customers in a new car. After interviewing about 120 car drivers, the team came out with the following chart of the customer requirements:

Desired Product Attributes in a New Car

Requirement	Rank
• Easy to drive	5
• Quiet riding, no squeaks or rattles	4.8
• Excellently finished	4.6
• Smooth riding even on rough road	4.5
• Excellent gas mileage	3.9
• Aerodynamic design	3.8
• Hugs the road	3.7
• Free from breakdowns	3.6
• Fast acceleration	3.5
• Virtually maintenance free	3.4
• Durable - will last 150000 miles	3.3
• Protects the driver and passenger in case of accident	3.2
• Classic styling	3
• Has instruments to read critical functions	2.2
• Has many electronic devises	2
• Has convertible roof	1.4

Translating into Technical Requirements

The product development team is all set to translate the requirements of the customers into technical requirements as per the QFD matrix.

Fallacy: The survey is based on aggregate data management. It assumes that there is one best solution for a customer need.

Classification of Needs

The CEO asks the product development team to classify the needs of the various customers into two different age groups and then give it a ranking, instead of proceeding simply on the basis of the aggregate data management. Accordingly, the product development team divided the customers into two broad categories:

1. Young drivers: Age group of 20 years to 35 years.

2. Old drivers: Age group of 35 years to 60 years.

The team then came with the following interesting findings:

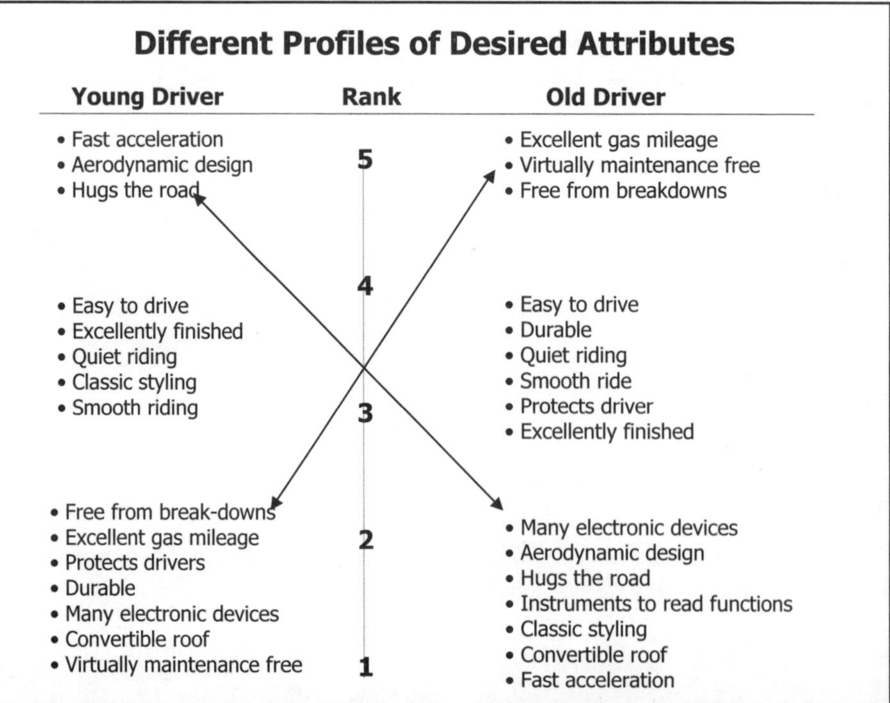

Customer Segmentation

- The classification of the customer requirements clearly reveals that the attribute which is the most important for the 'young driver', is least important for the 'old driver' and vice-versa.
- A simple listing of the customer requirements would have definitely ended up in the development of incorrect product for the market. Proper **customer segmentation** is, therefore, the most critical and challenging aspect of the whole QFD process.

Strengthening Internal Chain

Customer - Supplier Model

From the time an organization starts producing the products or services, to the time it delivers them to the external customers, the product or service goes through an internal chain of events. In that chain, everybody performs the role of a **customer, producer and supplier**.

Customer

When you accept the baton from a team mate you are a customer.

Producer

When you run with it for your leg of the relay, you are a producer - making some change or adding some value to the baton.

Supplier

Finally, when you pass the baton to the next member of the team, you become a supplier.

Final Outcome

The victory or the satisfaction of the external customer depends on how well the internal customer, producer & supplier have performed in the chain of events represented in a relay race.

Assessment of Internal Health of the Organization

OBJECTIVE

To strengthen internal customer - supplier chain for maximizing external customer satisfaction.

BUSINESS FUNCTIONS EXPECTATIONS

This assessment sheet contains expectations of the following business functions with each other. These expectations must be fully met for becoming a customer focused organization.

1 **HRD**
2 **Management Information Systems (MIS)**
3 **Accounts & Finance**
4 **Marketing**
5 **Production**
6 **Quality Assurance**
7 **Engineering**
8 **Purchase**

SCORE

The scores must be entered by the respective departments.
Enter your score on 1 to 5 scale.
(1 is the lowest and 5 is the highest satisfaction ratings)

1. HRD

	Expectations of User departments from HRD department.	Score
1	Recruitment and selection of right people.	
2	Timely placement & replacement of people.	
3	Facilitating training & development as per the business/job needs.	
4	Simple and user-friendly compensation package.	
5	Facilitating employees with residential accommodation & basic infrastructure.	
6	Taking good care of employee transportation, lunch and security.	
7	Career planning and growth of employees.	
8	To define & communicate all HR policies.	
9	To have well defined organization structure with clarity on authority and responsibility.	
10	Preparing employee welfare plans.	
11	To propagate reward schemes.	
12	To have transparent criteria for performance appraisal.	
13	Prompt & efficient handling of employee grievances.	
14	Decline in employee turnover ratio.	
15	Amicable and friendly relationships with labor unions.	
	Total	

	Expectations of HRD department from User departments.	Score
16	To receive proper manpower planning and budget in time.	
17	To receive required job profile / qualification & experience of the persons to be recruited.	
18	To receive specific requests for training and development.	
19	To adopt the value systems of the organization and to give their best to the organization.	
20	To receive periodic MIS from user depts.	
21	To receive the key result areas and targets of each employee from the departmental heads.	
22	To receive performance appraisals in time.	
23	To receive information on special/extraordinary performance by the employees.	
24	To receive exit interview reports from the user depts.	
	Total	

2. MIS

Expectations of User departments from MIS department.		Score
25	Providing latest hardware & technology to all users.	
26	Providing user friendly & efficient softwares for improving productivity.	
27	Providing real time and on-line information on all important business transactions.	
28	Providing tailor made software solutions to various departments.	
29	Alarming user depts. regarding any potential harm from virus etc.	
30	Taking preventive action for system maintenance.	
31	Promptly resolving complaints of user depts.	
32	Providing timely information to the decision makers.	
33	Easy flow of timely & accurate information and proper networking with other user departments.	
34	Maintaining up-to-date backup for all records.	
35	Contingency planning in case of system failure.	
36	Providing training & development to users on new softwares and keeping them updated.	
	Total	

Expectations of MIS department from User department.		Score
37	To receive information on specific hardware requirements.	
38	To receive information on specific software requirements.	
39	To give feedback on existing performance of the systems.	
	Total	

3. Accounts & Finance

Expectations of User departments from Accounts & Finance department.		Score
40	Efficient management of Working Capital.	
41	Preparing fund flow statements for atleast 6 months & taking proactive action for short falls.	
42	Preparing & communicating well defined financial authorities and responsibilities.	
43	Timely payment of employees salaries, reimbursements & disbursements.	
44	Timely payment to outside vendors & suppliers.	
45	Timely payment of statutory dues.	
46	Sending periodic information to all the employees regarding all advances & loans.	
47	Sending periodic information regarding age-wise account receivables status.	
48	Providing user departments with information on budget versus actual expenditure.	
49	Providing accurate and timely MIS.	
50	Prompt settlement of full & final cases.	
51	Giving advise on taxation matters to concerned employees.	
52	To co-ordinate with departmental heads for taking corrective action on findings of internal audit.	
	Total	

Expectations of Accounts & Finance department from User departments.		Score
53	Timely submission of employee's bill as per laid down policies of the company.	
54	Timely submission of vendor bills as per purchase policy.	
55	Prompt settlement of cash advances.	
56	Receiving prior information for making high value payments.	
57	Taking corrective action on the findings of the internal audit.	
58	Prompt realization of accounts receivables.	
59	Maintaining financial discipline and not to break various policies of the company.	
60	Take austerity measures and save money wherever possible.	
61	Adherence to all the financial norms laid down by the company in various manuals and policies.	
62	To spend company's money with due diligence.	
	Total	

4. Marketing - Production

Expectations of Marketing department from Production department.	Score
63 Supply of products conforming to customer's requirements.	
64 Defect-free production.	
65 Timely availability of finished products.	
66 Meeting quantity & time deadlines.	
67 Co-ordination with marketing people at the time of production planning.	
68 Intimating marketing department for any fluctuation in production costing well in advance.	
69 Intimating marketing department for any anticipated delays in meeting deliveries & other terms.	
70 Taking immediate action on the deficiencies in the products highlighted by marketing dept.	
Total	

Expectations of Production department from Marketing department.	Score
71 To provide realistic estimates of month to month marketing plans and sales forecasts.	
72 To intimate production dept. well in advance about major fluctuations in the marketing plan.	
73 To intimate production dept .regarding any specific / changed requirements of major customers.	
74 To receive periodic MIS regarding un-executed / cancelled orders.	
75 To provide continuous feedback on the performance of the product.	
76 To provide feedback on the performance of competitor's products.	
77 To facilitate involvement of important customers in the improvement plans if required.	
78 To be an integral part of product improvement plans.	
79 Not to put un-realistic time pressures.	
Total	

5. Production - Purchase

Expectations of Production department from Purchase department.	Score
80 To provide un-interrupted and timely supply of raw materials as per production plan.	
81 To ensure procurements as per specifications given by production & design dept.	
82 To provide good quality of raw materials / components.	
83 To arrange for materials immediately in case of sudden production demand.	
84 To involve production department while evaluating the supplier's capability.	
85 To enlist only those vendors who properly understand the requirements of production dept.	
86 To arrange for training and development of vendors in close coordination with production dept.	
87 To use feedback of production dept. in periodic performance evaluation of vendors.	
Total	

Expectations of Purchase department from Production department.	Score
88 Timely submission of a realistic production plan.	
89 To receive clear specifications of materials / components.	
90 To receive continuous feedback regarding quality of raw materials / supplier performance.	
91 To receive continuous feedback regarding excess re-work, scrap & wastage.	
92 To receive intimation for any major variations in the production plan.	
Total	

6. Production - Quality Assurance

Expectations of Production department from Quality Assurance department.	Score
93 Documenting quality system of the company with clear responsibility and authority.	
94 Timely receipt of inspection results.	
95 Timely authorization of product release.	
96 Effective participation in decisions relating to concessions in product conformance.	
97 Providing accurate assessment of causes of customer returns / complaints.	
98 Timely receipt of results on internal quality audits.	
99 Verification of corrective action.	
Total	

Expectations of Quality Assurance department from Production department.	Score
100 Allowing agreed time-frame for inspection / authorization / product release.	
101 Receipt of timely MIS on re-work, repairs and rejections.	
102 To follow defined processes, procedures and instructions.	
Total	

7. Production - Engineering

Expectations of Production department from Product Engineering department.	Score
103 Timely solution to problems relating to product engineering.	
104 Adequate availability of production facilities.	
105 Timely attendance of equipments faults / breakdowns.	
106 Scheduling preventive maintenance in consultation with production department.	
107 Assisting in reducing production, handling and set-up times.	
Total	

Expectations of Product Engineering department from Production department.	Score
108 Defining production process correctly.	
109 Making machines / equipments available for maintenance.	
110 Following recall schedules for jigs & fixtures and dyes.	
111 Not to over burden the machinery to meet the production targets.	
112 Ensuring self (operator) maintenance schedule.	
Total	

8. Quality Assurance - Purchase

Expectations of Quality Assurance department from Purchase department.		Score
113	To supply raw materials and components as per specifications given by QA.	
114	To involve QA department while evaluating the supplier's capability.	
115	To enlist vendors in close consultations / co-ordination with QA Dept.	
116	To involve QA dept. in training and development of vendors.	
117	To use QA dept. feedback as an integral part of performance evaluation of vendors.	
	Total	

Expectations of Purchase department from Quality Assurance department.		Score
118	To receive clear specifications of materials / components from QA.	
119	To receive MIS on supplier performance.	
120	To receive suggestions for improvement.	
	Total	

Analyze your total score:

0-240
Serious situation.

241-360
Average.

361-480
Good. You can do much better.

481-600
Excellent.
There is no room for complacency. Keep it up.

The word 'customer' historically derives from 'custom' meaning 'habit'. A customer was someone who frequented a particular shop, who made it a habit to purchase goods there and with whom the shopkeeper had to maintain a relationship to keep his or her 'custom', meaning expected purchases in the future.

"Sustained success means making the greatest possible impact over the longest period of time."

Marcus Buckingham - The One Thing You Need to Know.

Dramatic Difference

"Are you being reasonable? Most people are reasonable, that's why they only do reasonably well."

Paul Arden, Whatever You Think, Think the Opposite.

"The 'surplus society' has a surplus of **similar** companies, employing **similar** people, with **similar** educational backgrounds, coming up with **similar** ideas, producing **similar** things, with **similar** prices and **similar** quality."

Kjell Nordström - Funky Business

Decoding 'CUSTOMERS'

The word 'CUSTOMERS' stands for important excellence principles as shown below.

CUSTOMERS

CUSTOM

The customer should never give away his custom of buying products from you.

COMPETITIVE EDGE

As long as you provide the competitive advantages to your customers, they will remain loyal to you.

CUSTOMERS

• UNDERSTAND

Understand their stated and expected needs.

• UNPERCEIVED & UNARTICULATED

Translate their unperceived and unarticulated needs into new products & services for quantum jumps in business results.

CUSTOMERS

SERVICE

Set the standards for best performance. Make it a great experience and they will always remain loyal to you.

CUSTOMERS

•TANGIBLES

Nothing else matters for the customers. Tangibles comprise of product quality, design, features, performance & reliability. Provide your customers with tangibles that offers them maximum value.

•TIMELINESS

The customers count the speed of response time as the 'key value dimension'. They want everything 'RIGHT NOW'.

CUSTOMERS

OPPORTUNITY

They represent your biggest opportunity to grow. Nothing else matters. As long as you own the customer, you own the business.

CUSTOMERS

• MORE

They have to be given more and more. More quality, more choice, more features and more innovation.

• MOST IMPORTANT PERSON

Without any doubt, the customer is the most important person in business. Every thing else comes after the customer.

CUSTOMERS

• EXCELLENCE ALWAYS

Nothing less than 'Excellence' should be the goal. Provide your customers with products and services which have 'WOW' factors.

• EMPATHY

Put yourself in their shoes. Be your own customer periodically to find out the problems faced by your customers. Strive to remove all their problems, because all the problems will lead to shift in customer loyalty.

CUSTOMERS

RETENTION

It is very difficult to acquire the new customers. The cost of acquiring a new customer is 10 times more than the cost of retaining an old customer. The life long association of a customer with the organization translates into a very significant amount of money. Retain your customers at any cost.

CUSTOMERS

SUCCESS FACTORS

The success of your organization is guaranteed if you think of the customer's success factors. Move from customer satisfaction to 'customer's success'. Make products and services that will make your customers more and more successful every day.

5

Products & Processes

Toyota Production Systems

The World Drives Toyota

What drives Toyota?

Toyota is driven by the passion to create a better society.

A Passion to Create a Better Society

- Be a driving force in global re-generation by implementing the most advanced environmental technologies.
- Create automobiles and a motorized society in which people can live safely, securely and comfortably.
- Promote the advantages of cars throughout the world and attract more Toyota fans.
- Be a truly global company that is trusted and respected by all people around the world.

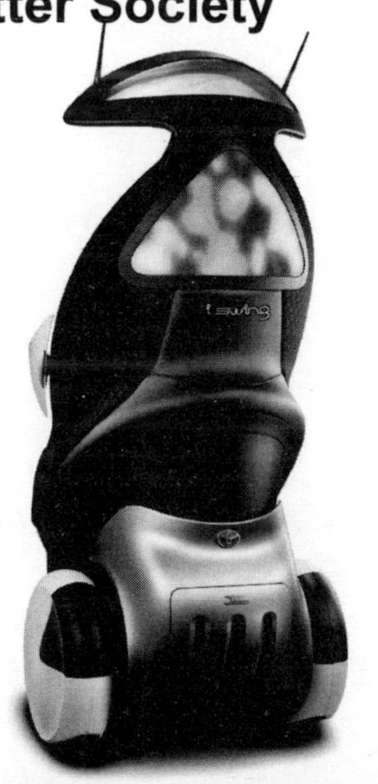

Monozukuri

Through 'Monozukuri' - manufacturing of value added products and technological innovation, Toyota is helping to create a more prosperous society. To achieve their objectives they follow the following key practices.

Key Toyota Practices

- **Excellence in DESIGN.**
- **Build quality into PROCESSES.**
- **Complete elimination of WASTE.**
- **Excellence in OPERATIONAL EFFICIENCY.**
- **LEAN manufacturing.**
- **Strive to be AHEAD of times.**

Note: The above points are separately mentioned in this section.

Toyota Production Systems

Toyota Production System

Toyota Motor Corporation's vehicle production system is a way of manufacturing products, which is referred to as 'Lean' Manufacturing System or 'Just-in-Time' (JIT) system.

Both Lean manufacturing and Just-in-time are recognized globally for maximizing operational efficiency.

Toyota Production System...

Toyota Production System has been established on the basis of many years of continuous improvements and research with the following two objectives:

1. Making the vehicles ordered by customers in the quickest and most efficient way.
2. To deliver the vehicles as quickly as possible to the customers.

Jidoka

The Toyota Production System (TPS) was established based on two concepts:

The first concept is called **'jidoka'** which can be loosely translated as **'automation with human reflexes'**. Jidoka blends robot technology with human behavior to prevent defective production.

Stop-in-Time

- Jidoka means that a machine automatically stops when the normal processing is completed.
- It also means that, should a quality or equipment problem arise, the machine detects the problem on its own and stops immediately, preventing the defective products from being produced. This prevents the cascading effects of defects.
- As a result, only products satisfying the required quality standards are be passed on to the next processes on the production line.

Built-in Quality

- Quality must be built-in during the manufacturing process. If a defective part or equipment malfunction is discovered, the machine concerned automatically stops and operators stop the work to correct the problem.
- For the effective functioning of 'Just-in-Time' system, all the parts in the production and assembly line must meet the pre-determined quality standards & specifications. This is achieved through jidoka.

Just-in-Time (JIT)

- The second concept of Toyota production systems is called 'Just-in-Time' (JIT). In JIT system, each process produces only what is needed by the next process in a continuous flow.
- Based on the scientific techniques of 'Jidoka' and 'Just-in-Time', the Toyota Production Systems can efficiently produce vehicles of excellent quality at the most competitive price for world-wide customer satisfaction.

JIT Production Systems

- JIT is a manufacturing technique based on planned elimination of all waste and continuous improvement of productivity. It encompasses the successful execution of all manufacturing activities required to produce a final product - from design engineering to delivery.
- The primary elements include having only the required inventory when needed; to improve quality to zero defects; to reduce lead time by reducing setup time, queue lengths and lot sizes; to incrementally revise the operations and to accomplish these objectives at minimum cost.

'Just-in-Time' Objectives

Making only

- Making only the desired product.
- At a desired time.
- In the desired quantity.

Fundamental Soul of Creation

"Design is the fundamental soul of a human made creation that ends up expressing itself in successive outer layers of the product or service."

Steve Jobs - CEO, Apple Computers

Functionality is
mundane,
Great designs
emote
desirability.

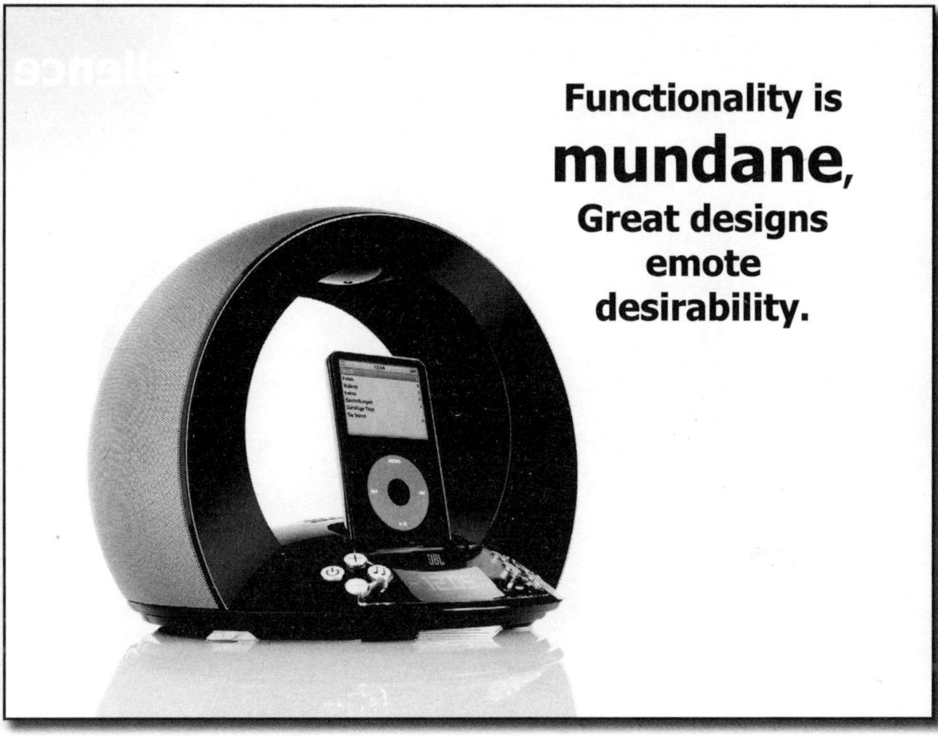

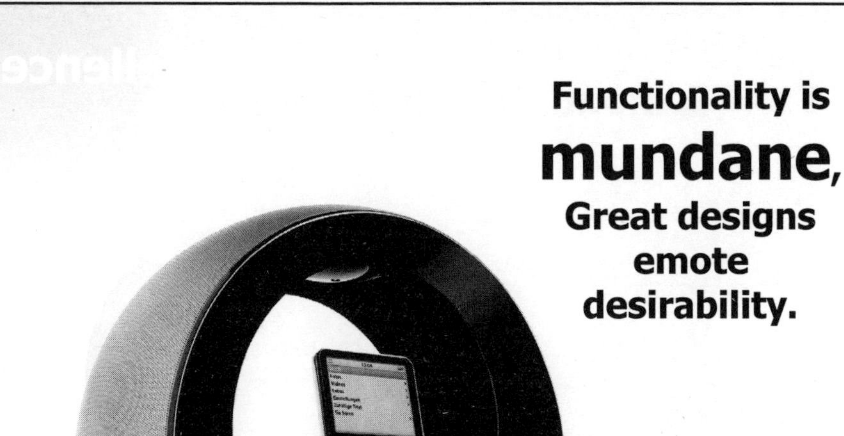

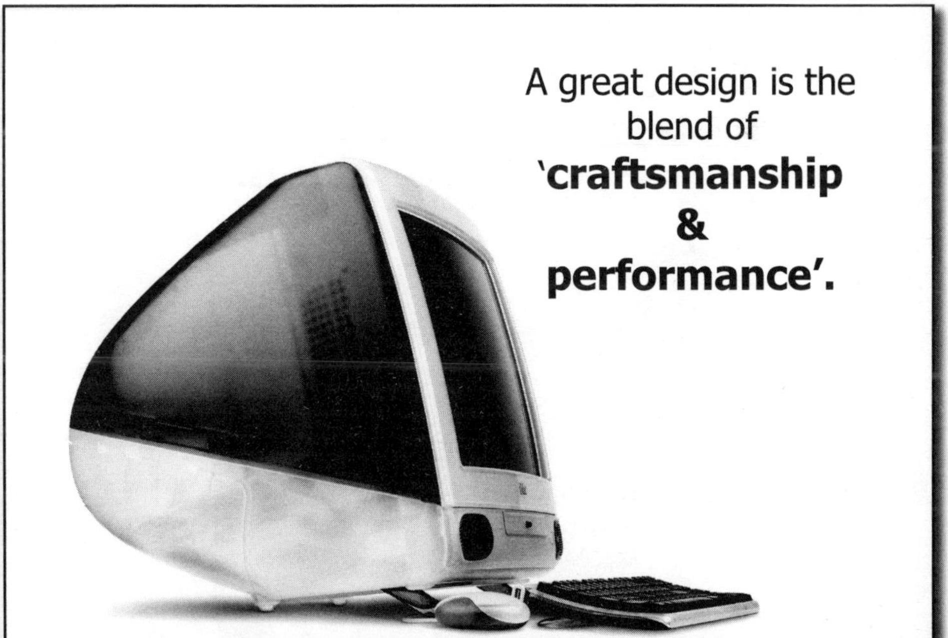
A great design is the
blend of
'craftsmanship
&
performance'.

A blend of 'arts & science'.

Design

The biggest source of sustainable competitive advantages.

Innovation in the context of new products is more focused on innovating 'NEW DESIGNS'.

The Differentiator

Consumers, who are choking on choice, look at design as the new differentiator. In a sea of look-alike products, a different design creates the 'Wow' factors for customers.

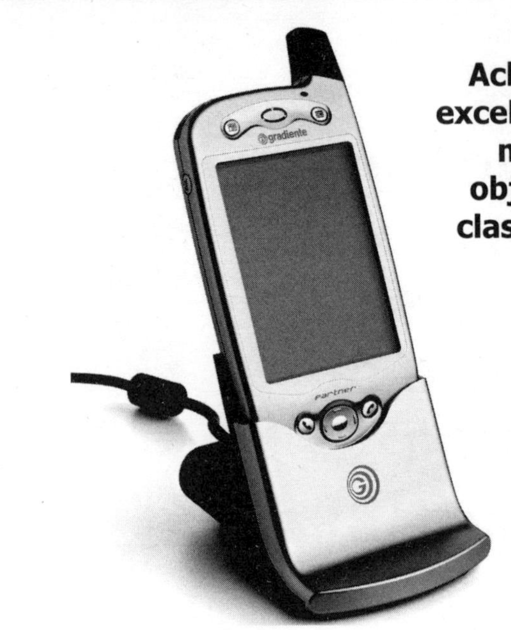

Achieving design excellence is one of the most important objectives of world class manufacturing.

Components of Great Designs

- Aesthetics – Wow factors
- Uncommon / Different / Stands out
- Enhances self-esteem
- Blend of craftsmanship & performance
- Creative
- Ergonomics – Space / Weight
- User-friendly
- Futuristic looks
- Attention to fine details

Design Principles

User Centered

Focuses on the needs, wants and limitations of the end user.

Use Centered

Focuses on how it will be used with less emphasis on the user and more emphasis on usage.

There is More Than One Way

This principle allows multiple ways of doing the same thing.

KISS Principle

Keep it smart and simple. This principle strives to eliminate unnecessary complications.

Murphy's Law

Everything that can go wrong will, therefore, plan for it beforehand.

Design & Reliability

Product Reliability

- Quality improvement has two faces - **internal and external**.
- Internal quality improvements deals with reduction of scrap, re-work, inspection costs etc.
- External quality improvement means enhancing the performance that the customers experience throughout the product's life span. It is very important to consider the reliability aspects while designing the new products.

Product Reliability...

- The major gains of external quality come from reduced field repairs, recalls, warranty, product re-design etc.

- Another benefit is the **increase in future sales** not only for the product in hand, but for the additional product the company manufactures. For example the improvement in the reliability of motorbikes can also favorably impact the company's sale of cars.

Top Priority

- Reliability has been defined as **quality over time**. It is the ability of the product to satisfactorily perform its designated function over its customer intended life time.
- Examples of unreliable products include inability of a product to function upon delivery, failure of a switching device to perform when called upon, premature changes in appearance, breakdowns etc.

Techniques

Reliability is the key element to quality improvement, it is often the part of quality that **affects the customers the most.** It is essential that management insists on comprehensive reliability improvement program at the product design stage itself.

Proactive

"If you need an equipment to improve the product reliability but don't buy it, you pay for it even though you don't have it." – **Henry Ford**

The most important goal of product life data analysis is proactive reliability improvement, preferably before the product release and at the **DESIGN stage** itself.

Conducting Failure Analysis

To improve reliability, one must understand the reason of failure. Once the process has been established and the machinery has been acquired and set up, it is extremely important to determine the failure modes and effects they have on the customer.

Period of Failure

- Engineers need to know in which **period of life** the part failed. Failures during the infant period may indicate a manufacturing defect rather than a reliability issue.
- Random failures during the useful life usually have other root causes, often correctable by **better design.**
- Failures at end of life may **indicate wear** and merit attention if they occur before the planned lifetime has passed.

Root Cause of Failure

Failure analysis strives to get to the root cause of the failure. Failure analysis reports should be well designed and integrated with the failure database. Design engineers should have a close working relationship with technicians performing failure analysis.

Highly Accelerated Life Testing (HALT)

- **Highly Accelerated Life Testing** (HALT) is becoming popular among reliability and design engineers for faster elimination of key failure modes before the product release.
- The objective of HALT application is to rapidly identify failures, which may require long time to discover under normal use conditions.
- Such testing is typically done on a few prototype units that are subjected to combinations of stresses at much higher levels than encountered in a normal operation.

Robust Design Experiments

Robust design experiments have great potential for improving products, process designs and reliability.

The key idea behind robust design methods is to choose the design conditions, which make the products robust to environmental factors. **Car crash tests** carried out by many automobile companies are good examples of testing robust designs in real conditions.

Product Reliability Measures

- Mean time to failure.
- Failure rate.
- Probability of failure occurrence during given time interval.
- Probability of failure non-occurrence during given time interval.
- Mean life time.
- Mean time to first generate overhaul.
- Mean time to repair.

Product Design Controls

Product design controls can be categorized in 3 parts:

1. **Knowing the product**
2. **Testing designs**
3. **Regulating designs**

1. Knowing the Product

Knowing the Product

- Do the designers know the multiple **applications** of the product?
- Do they have information on the **operating environments?**
- Do they have **access to the user** to discuss applications?
- Do they know the potential **field misuses** of the product?

Knowing the Product...

Do they have clear understanding of product requirement on:

- Performance
- Life
- Warranty period
- Reliability
- Maintainability
- Accessibility
- Safety
- Operating costs

Knowing the Product...

- Have the **non-quantitative** features of the product been defined in some manner?
- Do the designers know the level of product **sophistication** suitable for the user involved?
- Are adequate design guidelines, standards, handbooks and catalogues available?
- Do the designers understand the **interaction** of their part of design with remainder of the design?

Knowing the Product...

- Do the designers understand the **consequences of a failure** or other inadequacies of their designs on:
    1. The functioning of the total system
    2. Warranty costs and
    3. User costs ?
- Do they know the **relative importance** of various components & characteristics within components?
- Do the designers know what are the **manufacturing capabilities** relative to the design of tolerances?

2. Testing Designs

Testing Designs

- Do the designers have the means of **testing** their design with regard to the following:
  - a. Performance & reliability tests
  - b. Tests for unknown design interaction or effects
  - c. Pilot run
- Is their an **independent review** of design?
- Have the **detailed drawings** been checked?

Testing Designs...

- Do the designers record **analysis** for the design?
- Do the designers receive **adequate feedback** from development tests, manufacturing tests, acceptance tests and user experience?
- Are the **results quantified** where possible, including frequency of problems and costs to the manufacturer and user?

Testing Designs...

- Does the **failure information contain** sufficient technical details on causes?
- Are the designers aware of **material substitutions** or process changes?
- Do the designers receive **notice** when their designs specifications are not followed in practice?

3. Regulating Designs

Regulating Designs

- Have the designers been provided with the means of **regulating** the design process?
- Are they provided with the information on new **alternative materials** or design approaches?
- Have they been given the **performance information** on previous designs?
- Are the **results of research** efforts on new products transmitted to the designers?

Regulating Design...

- Are the **approvals** required from the designers to use products from the new suppliers?
- Do the designers participate in defining the criteria for **shipment** of the product?
- Can the designers **propose changes** involving trade-offs between functional performance, reliability and maintainability?

Regulating Design...

- Have the causes of **design failures** been determined by thorough analysis?
- Do the designers have the **authority** to follow their designs through the prototype stage and make design changes where needed?
- Can the designers **initiate design changes?**

Regulating Design...

- Are the **field reports reviewed** with designers before making decisions on design changes?
- Do the designers understand the **procedures** and chain of command for changing a design?

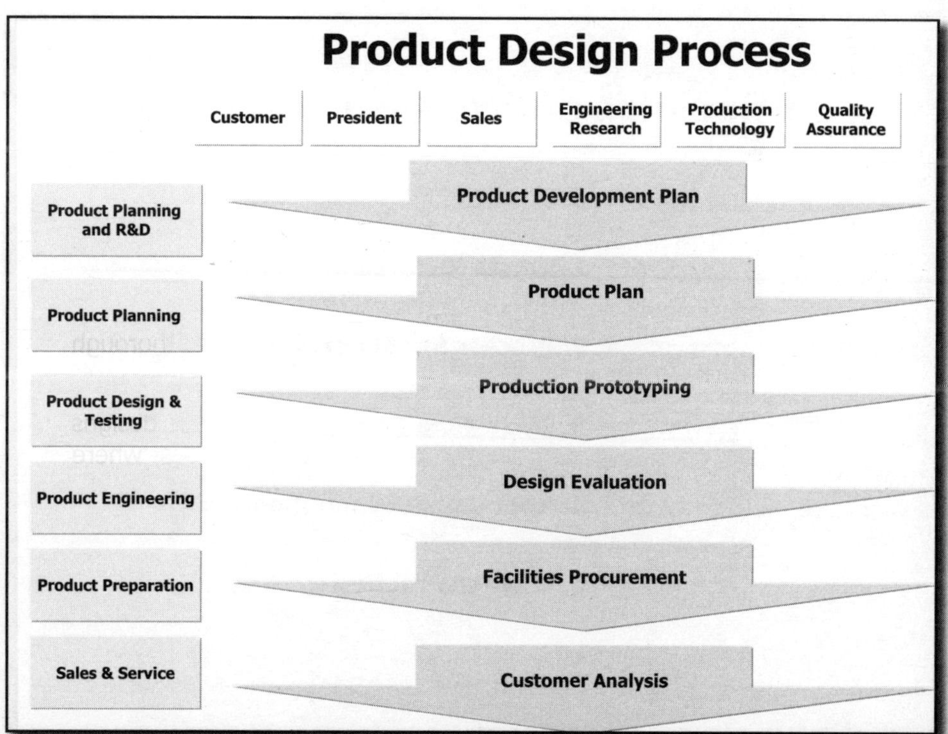

Process Excellence Principles

Principles of Process Excellence

1. Waste Reduction
2. Process Simplification
3. Cycle-time Reduction
4. Root Cause Elimination
5. Mistake Proofing

1.Waste Reduction

Waste is defined as any activity which CONSUMES RESOURCES but CREATES NO VALUE.

Types of Waste

- Waste of over production
- Waste of unnecessary inventory
- Waste of defects
- Waste of unnecessary motions
- Waste of in-appropriate processing
- Waste of waiting
- Waste of transporting
- Waste of untapped human potential
- Waste of in-appropriate systems
- Waste of energy & water
- Waste of material
- Service & office waste
- Waste of customer time
- Waste of defecting customers

Waste Reduction

Steps to waste reduction:

I. Value-added assessment

II. Minimize checks and inspections

III. Minimize administrative tasks

IV. Minimize storage and transportation activities

I. Value Added Assessment

Value Added Assessment...

Value to customer : First, the customer's view point should be considered. The customers are only interested in receiving the product or service that satisfies their requirements. All activities which are performed to cater to the customer's requirements are considered as **'value–added'** activities.

Value to Customer

- Would any customer care, if the activity was not performed?
- Would any customer object, if the activity was not performed?
- Do the customers appreciate the results of the activity?

Value to Business

There are many activities that may not add value from the customer's point of view. Attending meetings, developing plans, compliance with regulatory guidelines, writing procedures etc. are examples of activities that may not add value to the customers, but they do add value to the organization. Each of these activities must be carefully examined.

Reducing Non-Value Adding Activities

The organization must eliminate all the non-value adding activities from various processes and the time saved from these activities must be utilized for carrying out the improvement activities. A typical matrix of how the organization spends time is given below.

Non-Value Adding Activities

Improvement Activities

- Commitment to quality
- Customer driven approach
- Willingness to improve
- Effective problem solving
- Improvement targets
- Information sharing
- Company wide approach

Positive Activities

Dealing effectively with:-

- Customer queries
- Rush orders
- Surge of demand
- Staffing shortages
- Resource shortages

Negative Activities

- Avoiding quality problems
- Inter-departmental rivalry
- Secrecy
- Putting self needs before team needs
- Defensiveness

Ineffective Activities

- Chasing information
- Misdirected queries
- Unproductive meetings
- Seeking authority to act
- Bureaucracy
- Ineffective procedures

Matrix of Organizational Activities

Improvement Activities	**Positive Activities**
Time spent: 10%	Time spent : 60%
Negative Activities	**Ineffective Activities**
Time spent: 10%	Time spent: 20%

Reduce Time Spent on Negative & In-effective Activities

Improvement Activities	**Positive Activities**
Time spent: 40%	Time spent : 60%
Negative Activities	**Ineffective Activities**
Time spent: **nil***	Time spent: **nil***

*By eliminating the time spent on negative and ineffective activities, the organizations saves 30% time, which can be spent on improvement activities.

II. Minimize Checks and Inspections

Checks and inspections may be necessary in a process, however, they do not add value to the process. Each inspection point should be **identified and challenged**.

Minimize Checks and Inspections...

- What if the inspection was deleted?
- Would the inspection be missed?
- What is the potential impact in eliminating the inspection?
- What potential consequences exist, if the inspection is eliminated?
- What is the likelihood that the inspection would have revealed a problem?

III. Minimize Administrative Tasks

Administrative tasks often result in delays in process time due to excessive paper work, levels of reviews and multiple signatures. Reviews, approvals, signatures, preparing written documentation, making and distributing copies etc. needs to be thoroughly reviewed and kept to the minimum.

IV. Minimize Storage and Transportation Activities

Some transportation activities may be unnecessary and non-value adding. Often the relocation of an activity point can significantly reduce the transportation requirements.

2. Process Simplification

Process Simplification

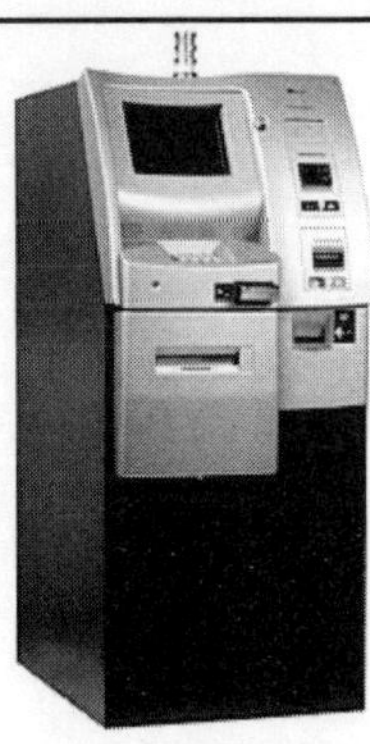

Simplification means **reducing the complexities** of the process. Simplification can lead to lesser activities and therefore, lesser things to go wrong. Process simplification can be done by combining similar activities and by analyzing various decision points.

Process Simplification

Old Process

Visit bank → Present cheque → Balance verification → Collect cash

Present cheque, Balance verification: **WASTE**

New Process

Visit ATM → Withdraw cash

Visit ATM → **Quality checks built-in**

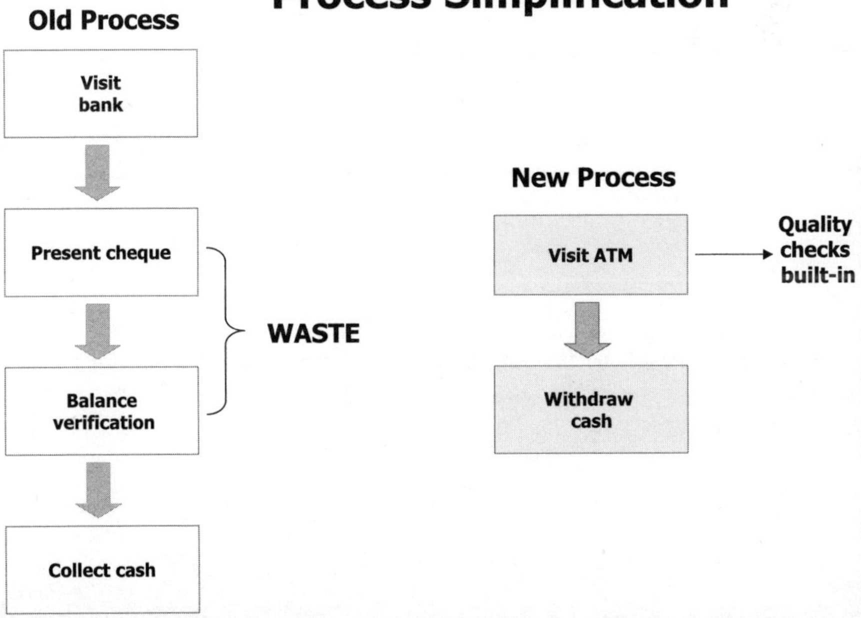

3. Cycle-time Reduction

Cycle-time Reduction

Cycle-time is defined as the duration from the initial expression of a customer's need, to the point when that need is satisfied. This cycle encompasses the entire value-added chain of a company's product or service delivery process. Longer cycle-times not only prevent prompt delivery of product / service to your customers, but also increase costs.

Key Value Dimension

- Customers now penalize suppliers that infringe on their time, whether through delays, mistakes or inconveniences. Today's customers demand operations that are airborne, on-line and real-time. 'Soon' is not the answer the customers want to hear.
- They count the speed of response time as a **Key Value Dimension**. Their directive to the market place is loud and clear - continuously shrink the interval between our need and when you can fill it - qualitatively.

Cycle-time Reduction

Broadly speaking, an organization competes on the basis of quality, cost, flexibility and time. Today's discriminating customer demands world-class quality at a competitive price and in the fastest possible time. Many companies confine the cycle-time only to the production systems. There are other categories of cycle time, which must be reduced to maximize the overall operating efficiency.

Various Cycle-times

- **Production cycle-time** - Raw materials to final product.
- **Purchase cycle-time** - Indent to items in house.
- **Marketing cycle-time** - Sales to money in bank.
- **Recruitment cycle-time** - Vacancy to actual joining.
- **Innovation cycle-time** - Opportunity evaluation to new products.
- **Product Engineering cycle-time** - Prototype to finished product.
- **Quality Assurance cycle-time** - Defects to error free products.

Strategic Weapon

Cycle-time can be used as a strategic weapon for:

- Gaining competitive advantages.
- Identifying new markets and opportunities.
- Responding to those opportunities before the competitors.

4. Eliminating Root Causes

Eliminating Root Causes of Critical Business Problems

Root Cause Analysis is a scientific method of resolving business problems. The practice of Root Cause Analysis is predicated on the belief that problems are best solved by attempting to correct or eliminate root causes, as opposed to merely addressing the immediately obvious symptoms.

Root causes of some of the important business problems are shown in the following figures.

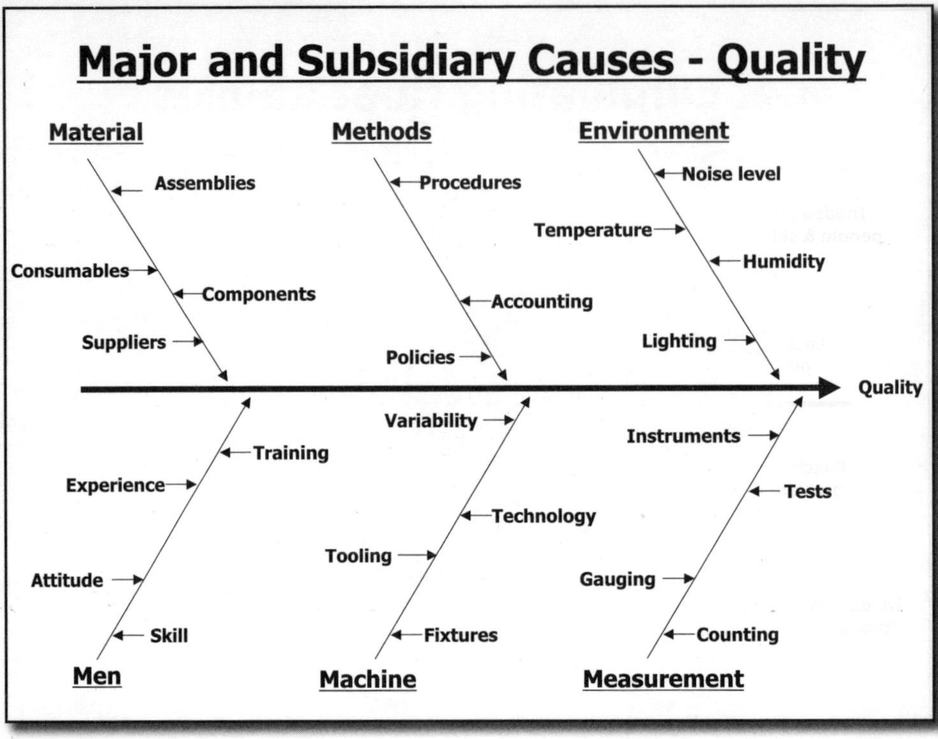

Major and Subsidiary Causes - Quality

Material
Assemblies
Consumables
Components
Suppliers

Methods
Procedures
Accounting
Policies

Environment
Noise level
Temperature
Humidity
Lighting

Quality

Men
Training
Experience
Attitude
Skill

Machine
Variability
Technology
Tooling
Fixtures

Measurement
Instruments
Tests
Gauging
Counting

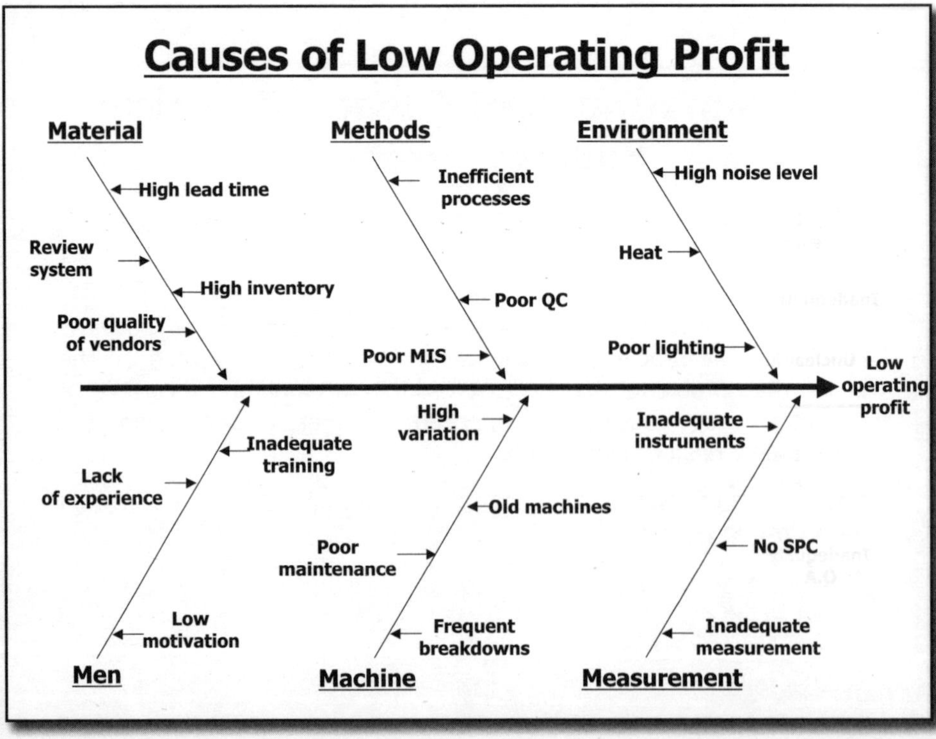

Causes of Low Operating Profit

Material
High lead time
Review system
High inventory
Poor quality of vendors

Methods
Inefficient processes
Poor QC
Poor MIS

Environment
High noise level
Heat
Poor lighting

Low operating profit

Men
Inadequate training
Lack of experience
Low motivation

Machine
High variation
Old machines
Poor maintenance
Frequent breakdowns

Measurement
Inadequate instruments
No SPC
Inadequate measurement

Causes of Low Market Share

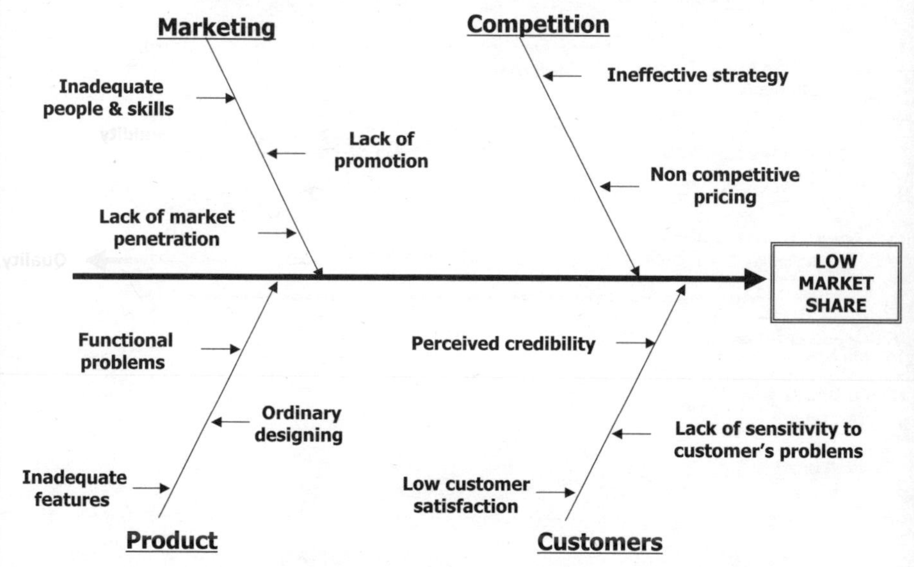

Marketing
- Inadequate people & skills
- Lack of promotion
- Lack of market penetration

Competition
- Ineffective strategy
- Non competitive pricing

Product
- Functional problems
- Ordinary designing
- Inadequate features

Customers
- Perceived credibility
- Lack of sensitivity to customer's problems
- Low customer satisfaction

LOW MARKET SHARE

Causes of Low Productivity

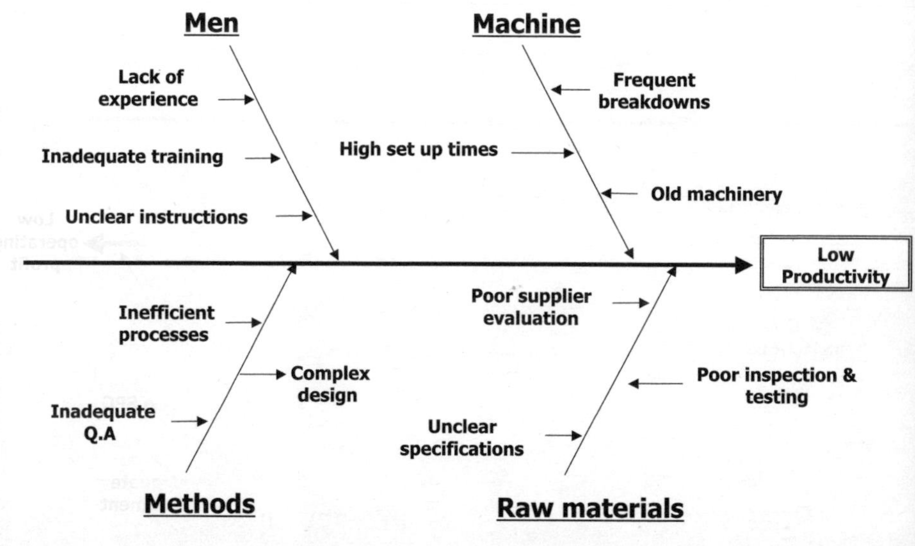

Men
- Lack of experience
- Inadequate training
- Unclear instructions

Machine
- Frequent breakdowns
- High set up times
- Old machinery

Methods
- Inefficient processes
- Complex design
- Inadequate Q.A

Raw materials
- Poor supplier evaluation
- Poor inspection & testing
- Unclear specifications

Low Productivity

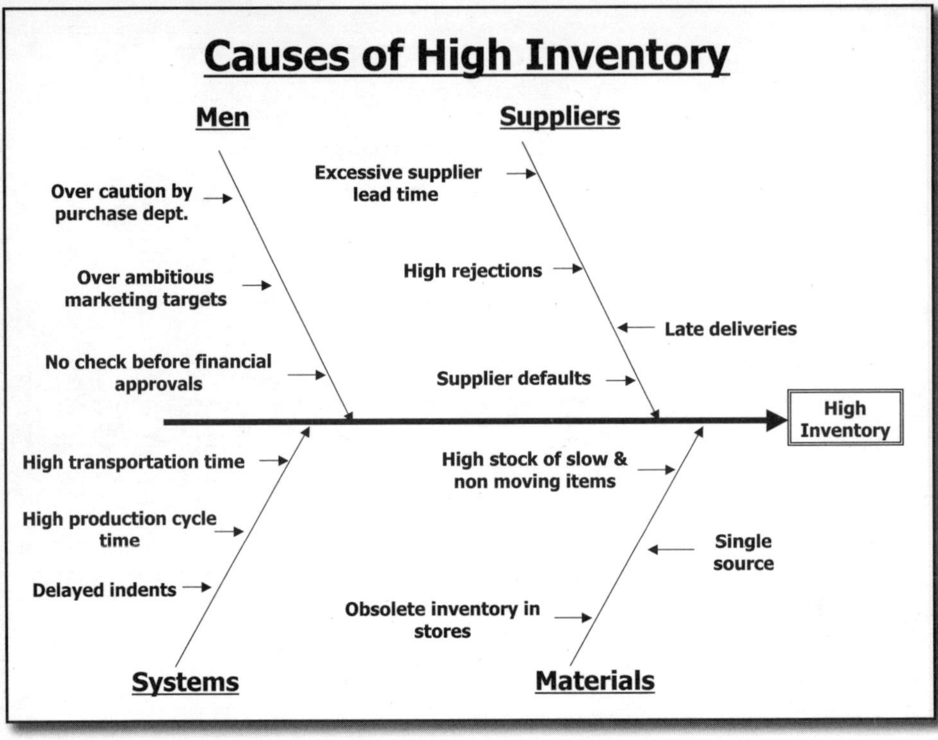
Causes of High Inventory
Men
Suppliers
Over caution by purchase dept.
Over ambitious marketing targets
No check before financial approvals
Excessive supplier lead time
High rejections
Late deliveries
Supplier defaults
High Inventory
High transportation time
High production cycle time
Delayed indents
High stock of slow & non moving items
Single source
Obsolete inventory in stores
Systems
Materials

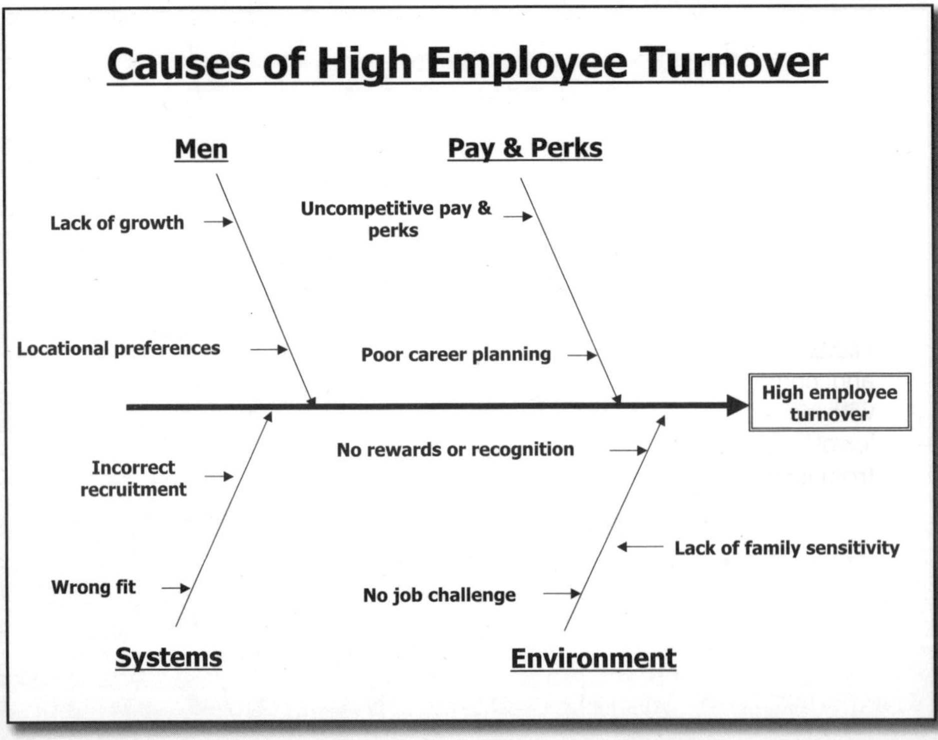
Causes of High Employee Turnover
Men
Pay & Perks
Lack of growth
Locational preferences
Uncompetitive pay & perks
Poor career planning
High employee turnover
Incorrect recruitment
Wrong fit
No rewards or recognition
Lack of family sensitivity
No job challenge
Systems
Environment

Mistake Proofing

Mistake proofing is a scientific technique for improvement of products and operating systems, (including materials, machines and methods) with an aim of preventing problems due to **human errors.** The term 'error' means a sporadic deviation from standard procedures resulting from loss of memory, perception or motion.

Requirements

- Inspection processes or the use of statistical control should be **completely eliminated**.
- Quality should be controlled at the **source of the problem** and not after the problem has manifested itself.
- Inspection should be **incorporated within the process** and at the point where the problem has been identified.

Principles of Mistake Proofing

A. Prevention of Occurrence

Methods under this principle aim to prevent the occurrence of human errors from all stages of operations and make corrections unnecessary. This can be done through the following 3 methods:

I. Elimination

II. Replacement

III. Facilitation

I. Elimination

- Elimination method aims to **remove the system properties** which generate operations / restrictions susceptible to human errors so as to make them unnecessary.
- Consider the error of an operator touching a high temperature pipe and getting burnt. One method of preventing this error is to make the pipe safe by covering it with insulating material.

II. Replacement

Replacement method substitutes a more reliable process to improve the consistency of processes. For example the use of robotics or automation prevents the manual assembly error. Similarly automatic dispensers or applicators ensure that the correct amount of a material is applied.

III. Facilitation

The purpose of facilitation is to design the work stations or production cells in such a manner so that it becomes easier for the workers to perform their designated tasks without any error of **memory, perception and motion.** Good visual controls, availability of right tools, well trained people and clear instructions at the designated work stations facilitate error-free production.

B. Minimization of Effects*

Methods under this principle aim to minimize the effects of human error and focus on processes where the errors develop into serious problems of quality, safety or efficiency. This can be divided into two categories:

I. Detection

II. Mitigation

***This principle is also known as 'Stop-in-Time'.**

I. Detection

Under this principle, even if a human error occurs, the deviations from the standard states caused by it can be detected and corrected in the succeeding operation steps. The methods of correcting the detected deviations are classified into two types :

1. Operators are **informed** or find by themselves the deviations and take necessary corrective action.

2. The deviations are **automatically corrected** without operators.

Prevention of Defects

Cause | **Intermediate Result** | **End Result**

Work method → Machine or human error → Detect error → Take corrective action → Zero Defects

Take corrective action → Analyze for preventive action → Modify work procedure to prevent such errors → Work method

II. Mitigation

The mitigation method aims to make **operations redundant** or incorporate shock absorbing / protecting materials so as to mitigate the effects of human errors in their development process.

Example: Consider the error of burning out the motor of a production machine by forgetting to switch off the power supply. The mitigation counter-measure is to install a fuse, which cuts off the power supply when the temperature reaches a certain point.

Six-Sigma

- Six-Sigma is a scientific approach for maximizing the overall business results. It is a methodology driven by understanding customer needs and the disciplined use of data, facts and statistical analysis to improve the organizational processes, products and financial performance.
- Statistically, Six-Sigma means six standard deviations from the mean. It is a measure of quality that strives for near perfection. To achieve Six-Sigma, a process should not produce more than 3.4 defects per million opportunities.
- Six-Sigma methodology need not be confined to manufacturing processes – It can be effectively used to maximize the performance of other business functions like marketing, HR and service industries as well.

Sigma Levels and Defect Rate

Quality Level	% Quality	Defective PPM*
3 Sigma	99.73	66807
4 Sigma	99.9937	6210
5 Sigma	99.999943	233
6 Sigma	**99.9999998**	**3.4**

***Parts Per Million**

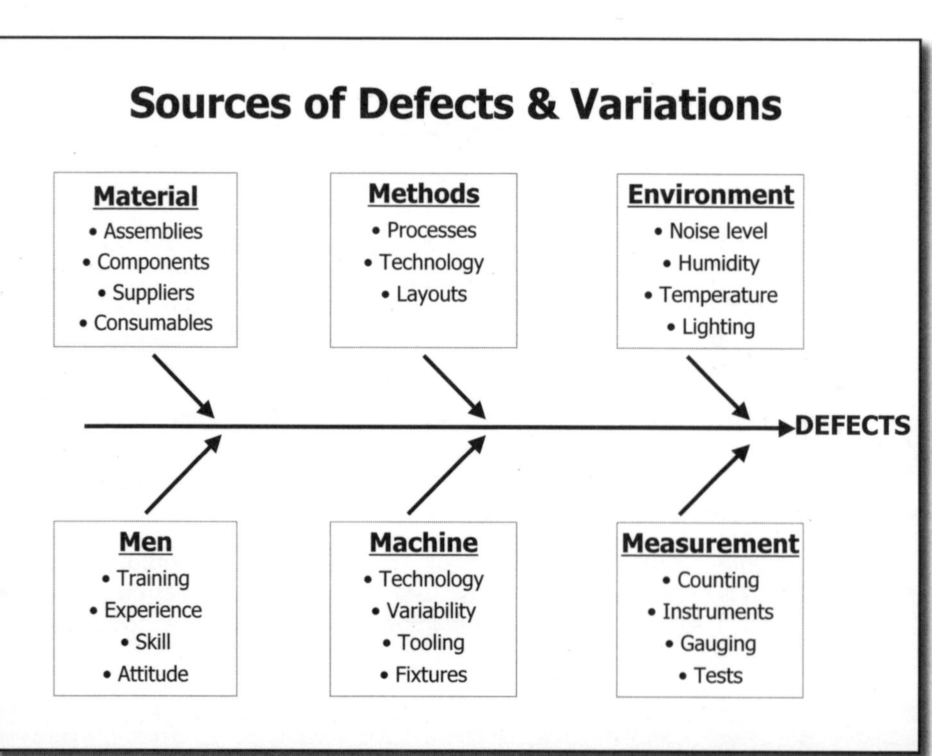

Sigma Levels & Cost of Quality

Sigma	Defect Rate(PPM)	Cost of Quality as % of Turnover	Competitive Level
6	3.4	<10%	World Class
5	233	10-15%	
4	6210	15-20%	Industry Average
3	66807	20-30%	
2	308537	30-40%	Non-competitive
1	6,90000	>40%	

Objectives of Six-Sigma

- Customer value enrichment.
- Process improvement.
- Defects reduction.
- Top-line & Bottom-line improvement.

Six-Sigma in Statistical Terms

- The term **'Sigma'** taken from the Greek alphabet, is used to designate measure of variation from the mean. It represents the distribution or **spread** of the mean (average) of any parameter of product, process or procedure.
- In the context of business or manufacturing process, Sigma capability is a metric which indicates how the process is behaving. The higher is the Sigma value, the better is the capability of a process to produce defect free work and vice-versa. The spread of various sigma levels is shown below:

3 Sigma Vs. 6 Sigma

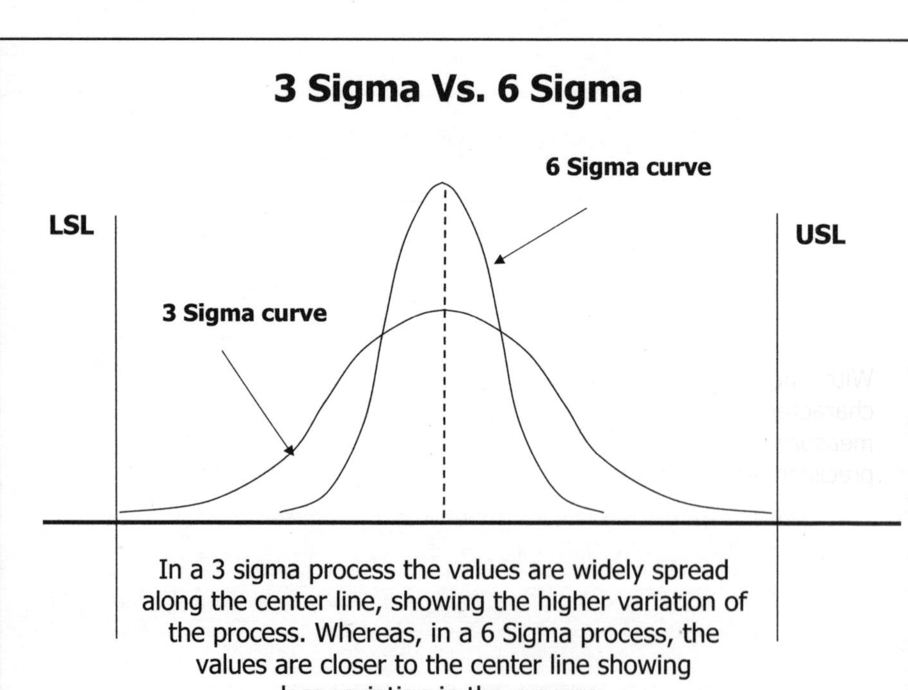

In a 3 sigma process the values are widely spread along the center line, showing the higher variation of the process. Whereas, in a 6 Sigma process, the values are closer to the center line showing less variation in the process.

Six-Sigma in Simple Terms

Six-Sigma can be best explained by using the analogy of a rifle firing at a target.

Accuracy and Precision

With the center of the target taken to be the true value of the characteristic being measured and the rifle shots representing the measured values, there are four combinations of accuracy and precision as depicted below:

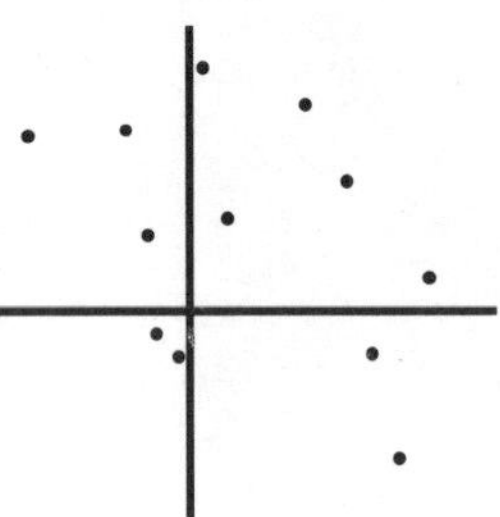

Accurate but Imprecise

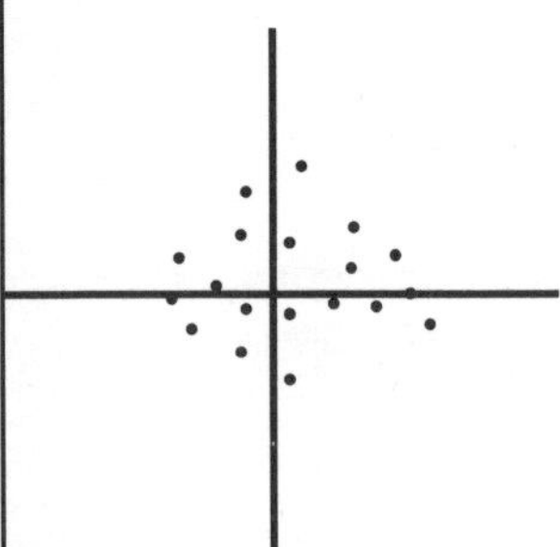

Precise but Inaccurate

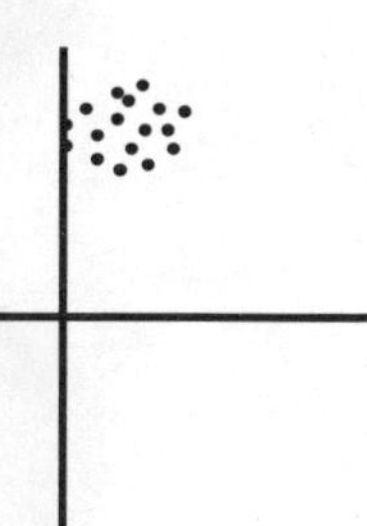

Accurate and Precise

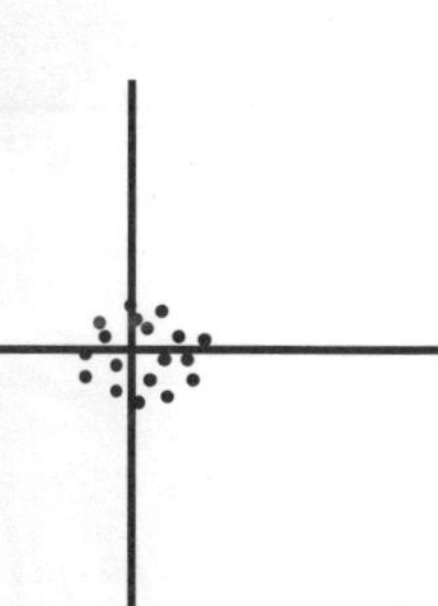

Six-Sigma DMAIC Strategy

DMAIC

DMAIC is a systematic approach for improving the products, processes and business results. It is an integral part of the Six-Sigma breakthrough strategy. DMAIC is the acronym for 5 phases of Six-Sigma – Define, Measure, Analyze, Improve and Control.

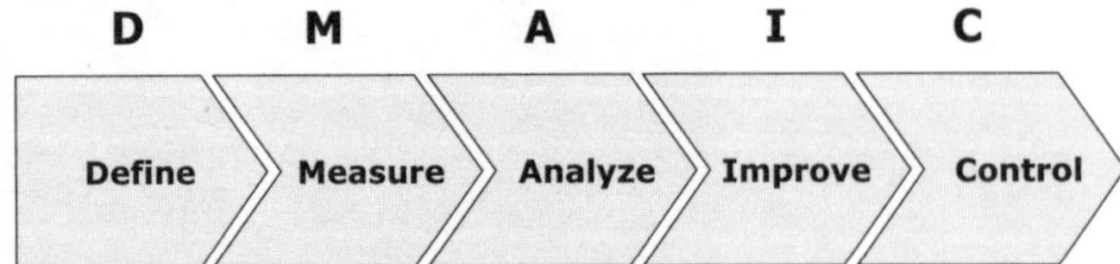

DMAIC Focus

The DMAIC strategy should be selected on the basis of any of the following criteria:

- **Maximizing customer values.**
- **Improving process efficiency.**
- **Maximizing top-line and bottom-line.**

Define

This phase **defines the project**. It identifies critical customer requirements and links them to business needs. It also defines a project charter and the business processes to be undertaken for Six-Sigma.

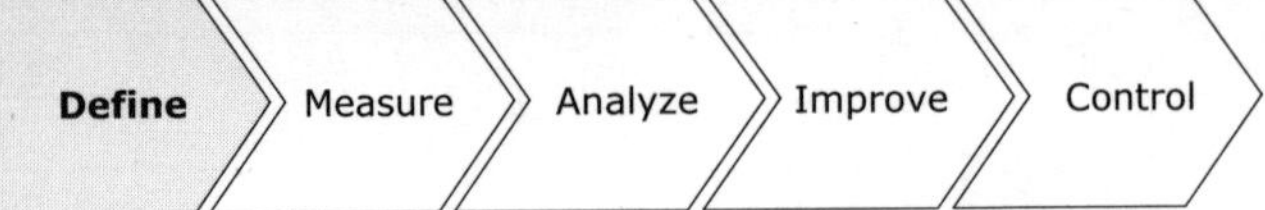

Steps

A. Identify projects critical to customers & business:

- Products
- Processes
- Market share / Profits

B. Define process map:

- Key processes for achieving Six-Sigma projects
- Inputs
- Outputs

C. Develop action plan:

- Project deliverables with time frame
- Roles & responsibilities

Tools & Techniques

- Project charter
- Customer surveys
- Comment cards
- Lost customer / Customer dissatisfaction analysis
- Process map
- Quality Function Deployment (QFD)*
- Benchmarking

*Refer to QFD in 'Customers' section for more details.

Measure

This phase involves selecting the product characteristics, mapping respective process, making necessary measurements and **recording the results** of the process. This is essentially a data collection phase.

Steps

- Identify key business performance measures*.
- Identify key process measures.
- Measure present level of defects, capability and sigma levels.
- Identify key input, processes and output variables.
- Measure current process performance in terms of capability indices.
- Measure current process performance in terms of yield.

*Refer to 'Measures of Excellence' at the end of this section.

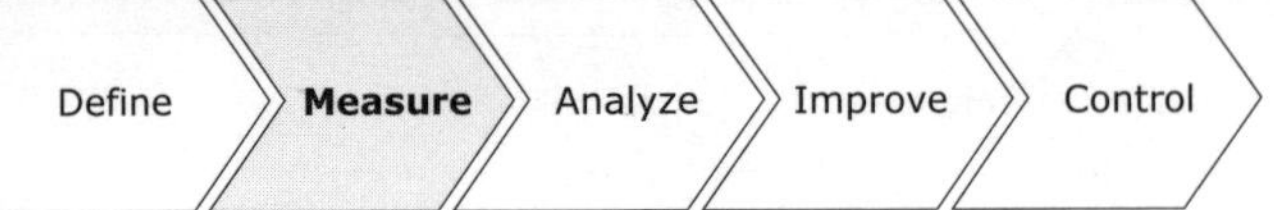

Tools & Techniques

- Measurement systems analysis
- Annual financial reports
- Process capability indices
- Process behavior charts - SPC
- Exploratory data analysis
- Descriptive statistics
- Data mining
- Pareto analysis

Analyze

In this phase an action plan is created to close the **'gap'** between the present performance and the targeted performance.

Steps

- Identify gaps between current level of performance and the desired level of performance.
- Generate list of possible causes and sources of defects.
- Prioritize list of 'vital few' causes of defects and variation.
- Identify the root causes of problems.
- Identify present levels of cost of poor quality.
- Quantify present investment and future financial savings.
- Prepare an action plan for closing the gap between present performance and desired performance.

Tools & Techniques

- Cause-and-effect diagrams
- Tree diagrams
- Brainstorming
- Benchmarking studies
- Process Maps
- Design of Experiments
- Failure Mode and Effect Analysis (FMEA)
- Simulation

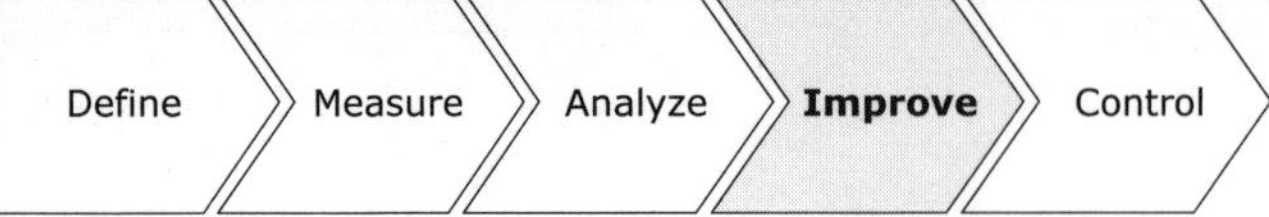

Improve

This phase involves **improving processes / product** performance characteristics for achieving desired results and goals. This phase involves application of scientific tools and techniques for making tangible improvements in profitability and customer satisfaction.

Note: Refer 'Process Excellence Principles' mentioned earlier in this section.

Steps

- Benchmark products with the best-in-class.
- Select best options for improvement.
- Allocate resources for meeting objectives.
- Improve products for value enrichment for customers.
- Improve product designs.
- Reliability improvement.
- Improve key business processes to deliver speed, service & quality.
- Technology up-gradation.
- Mistake proofing with built-in quality features.
- Implement improvement plans.

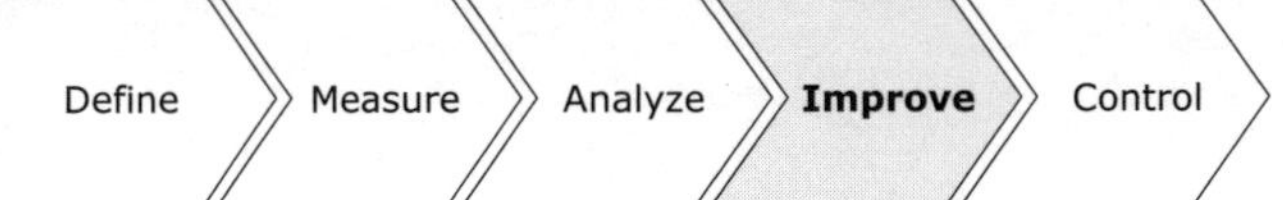

Tools & Techniques

- Quality Function Deployment (QFD)*
- Design of experiments (DOE)
- Failure Mode and Effect Analysis (FMEA)
- Business Process Re-engineering
- Project planning and management tools
- Prototype and pilot studies
- Cause & Effect analysis

*Refer to QFD in 'Customers' section for more details.

Control

This phase requires the process conditions to be properly documented and monitored through various control methods so that the results are sustained in the long run and do not deviate or slip-back.

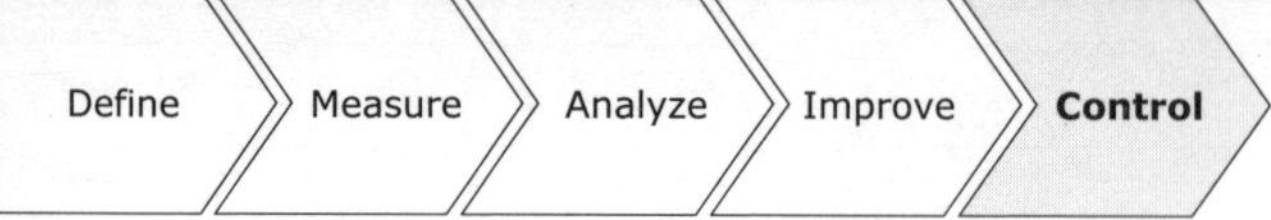

Steps

- Ensure that control plans are in place for smooth operations.
- Establish contingency plans.
- Document new operating procedures.
- Ensure that new process steps, standards and documentation are integrated into routine operations.
- Ensure that all control mechanisms are deployed and understood.

Tools & Techniques

- Statistical Process control charts
- FMEA
- Mistake proofing
- Risk management

The Breakthrough Strategy

The power of DMAIC methodology lies in the **structure and rigor**. Each phase is designed to ensure that:

- Organizations apply the breakthrough strategy in a systematic way.
- Six-Sigma projects are systematically designed and executed.
- The results of these projects are incorporated into business.

Strategy at Various Levels

Almost every organization can be divided into 3 basic levels:

1. Business level

2. Operations level

3. Process level

It is extremely important that Six-Sigma is understood and integrated at every level in the organization.

DMAIC – Multiple Applications

- Executives at the **business level** can use DMAIC strategy for improving the market share, profitability and long term viability.
- Managers at **operations level** can use DMAIC to improve yield and reduce various costs.
- At the **process level** engineers can use DMAIC to reduce defects and variation for improving process capability, leading to better customer satisfaction.

Business Perspective of DMAIC

- **Define** the business plans for making improvement.
- **Measure** the business systems that support the plans.
- **Analyze** the gaps in system performance benchmarks.
- **Improve** system elements to achieve performance goals.
- **Control** system-level characteristics that are critical to value.

Operations Perspective of DMAIC

- **Define** projects to resolve operational issues.
- **Measure** the current performance of the operations.
- **Analyze** project performance in relation to operational goals.
- **Improve** the operations with focus on speed, service & quality.
- **Control** inputs and outputs of the operations.

Process Perspective of DMAIC

- **Define** the processes that contribute to the functional problems.
- **Measure** the capability of each process.
- **Analyze** the data to assess prevalent patterns and trends.
- **Improve** the key business processes.
- **Control** the process variables that exert undue influence.

LEAN Manufacturing System (LMS)

Lean Manufacturing System

Lean Manufacturing System is a technique for maximizing operational efficiency and customer value by:

- Using the least amount of human effort, space, resources and time.
- Improving production flow – A line synchronization method to make the product flow through various stages, without any interruption.
- Implementing 'Pull' systems – The flow of resources in a production process by replacing only what has been consumed.

Focus of Lean Manufacturing

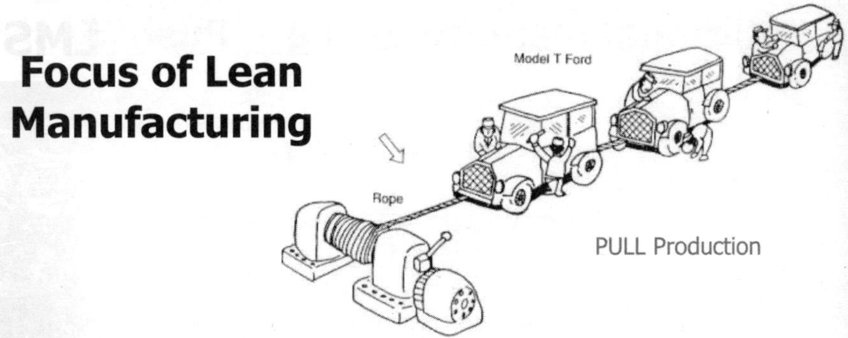

Lean Manufacturing System focuses on identifying and eliminating all kinds of waste and non-value added activities from the manufacturing processes to improve:

- **Quality**
- **Cost**
- **Delivery**

7 Types of Waste

1. Non-standardization and variation in production processes.

2. Inadequate capacity utilization.

3. Waiting time of men, machines and materials.

4. Unnecessary movement of material.

5. Pre-process and in-process inventory.

6. Excessive cycle-time and consumption of materials.

7. Producing defective goods and unnecessary.

Traditional Manufacturing - 'Push' System

Starts in factory

- Production plan based on demand forecast
- Material procurement to meet production plan
- Material receipt and inspection
- Storage of materials and components till required for processing
- Actual production
- Storage of components required for assembly
- Assembly, final inspection and packaging
- Storage of finished goods in warehouses
- On the shelf in retail outlets

↓

Ends with the customer

Weakness of Traditional System

- Risk related to forecasts.
- Long overall business process cycle.
- Good comfort level at various stages, leading to slack in the system.
- Hides the problems, waste and obstacles in the business flow.
- Encourages un-healthy departmental focus.

Resulting in increased costs.

Optimum Utilization

Lean Manufacturing Systems aims at optimum utilization of:

- **Time:** By improving cycle-time across the value chain.
- **Space:** By reducing inventory.
- **Men:** By improving the skill base and productivity.
- **Materials:** By maximizing process efficiency & yield.
- **Money:** By eliminating all kinds of waste.
- **Machines:** By maximizing equipment efficiency through TPM*.

*** Refer next chapter on Total Productive Maintenance (TPM).**

Lean Manufacturing - 'Pull' System

Starts with customer

↓

- Order acquisition by marketing
- Production planning
- 'Just-in-time' receipt of material
- 'Pull system' of production – Followed by the entire process chain by kanban (visual controls)

↓

Ends with primary producers

Key Principles of LEAN

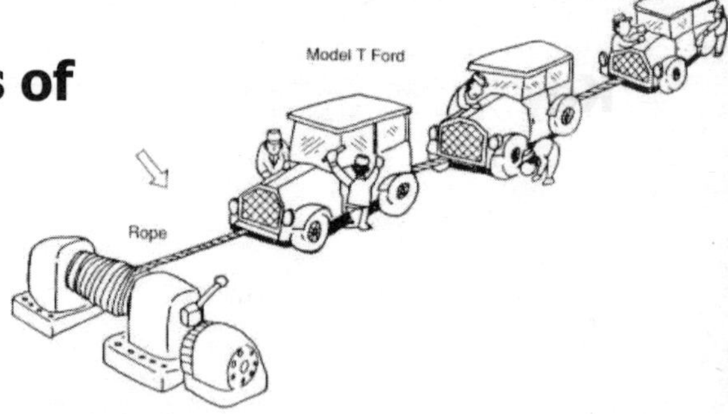

- **Minimize material handling:** Preference should be given to low or no cost solutions. Efforts should be made to handle the products only once.
- **Minimize distances:** Avoid walking and carrying materials and components by creating cells, combining operations within a work center and better space planning.

Key Principles...

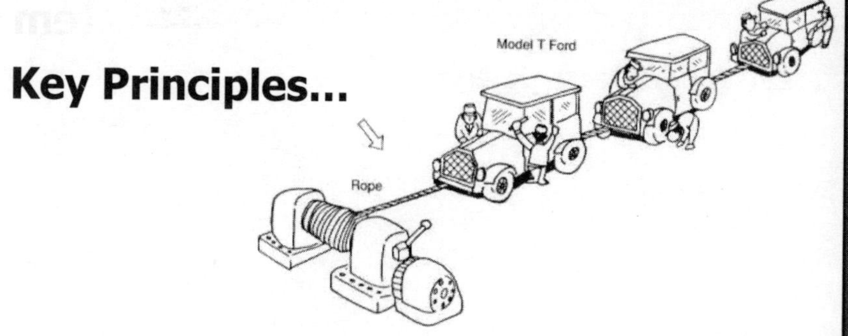

- **Minimize strain:** Work centres should be ergonomically designed to avoid back and other muscle strains.
- **Minimize clutter:** Everything must be in the designated place and there should be a place for everything.
- **Minimize storage:** If you have the space, it will surely get filled. Continuously minimize the storage space for raw material, WIP, finished goods and spare parts throughout the supply chain.

Key Principles...

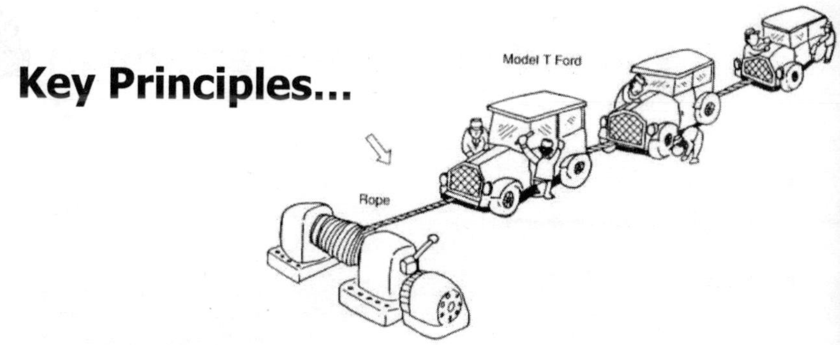

- **Maximize utilization:** Make optimal use of people, space and equipment to improve the return on investment.
- **Maximize flexibility:** The key to lean manufacturing is creating a layout that can adapt quickly to changes in product, equipment, personnel and material.
- **Maximize smooth flow:** Continuously determine and eliminate the bottlenecks to ensure smooth production flow.

Key Principles...

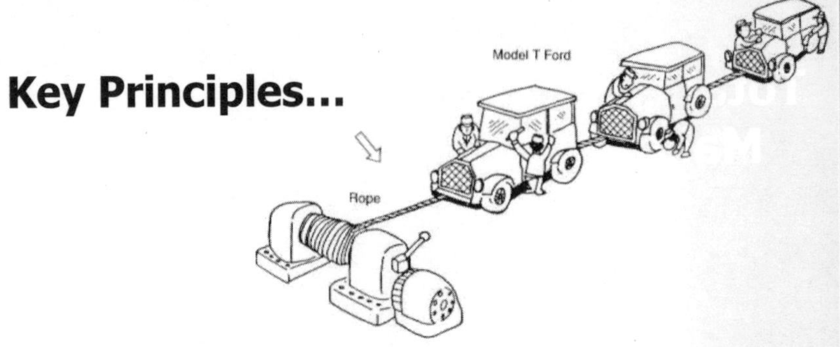

- **Maximize visibility:** To quickly spot the problems, maintain a clear line of vision to 'anywhere from anywhere'. Work centres must have good visual controls to avoid human errors.
- **Maximize communication:** Lean manufacturing requires a regular feedback on the operations for making continuous improvements.

Tools of Lean Manufacturing

- JIT
- Total productive maintenance
- Process optimization
- Visual controls
- Streamlined layout
- Batch size reduction
- Point of use storage
- Quick changeover
- Mistake proofing

TPM - A Zero Sum Game

- **Zero Unplanned Down-time**
- **Zero Defects**
- **Zero Speed Losses**
- **Zero Accidents**

TPM – Key Requirement of Lean Manufacturing

- **'Lean Manufacturing'** requires 100% machine time availability for optimizing process efficiency and producing quality products at lower operating costs.
- Quality, cost and timely delivery increasingly depend on equipment conditions.

If your equipment won't run, nothing else matters!

Goals & Objectives

- To get the most efficient use of all the production equipments.
- To establish a Total (company wide) Productive Maintenance.
- To achieve full participation of equipment designers and engineers, equipment operators and maintenance department personnel.

TPM Targets
"6 Big Machine Losses"

1. Unexpected breakdowns.
2. Set-up and adjustments (Changeover).
3. Minor stoppages.
4. Actual operating speed versus designed speed.
5. Defects and re-working of defects.
6. Reduced yield between start of production and stable production.

The TPM Paradigm Shift

Old Fashioned Attitude

- **"I operate, you fix"**
- **"I fix, you design"**
- **"I design, you operate"**

TPM Approach

"We are all responsible for our equipments."

TPM
Roles & Responsibilities

- **Who does what?**
- **When do they do it?**
- **Why do they do it?**
- **How do they do it?**
- **For how long they do it?**

The Operator's Role

- Perform basic equipment maintenance cleaning of machines.
- Maintain proper equipment condition.
- Diagnose & perform repairs for some problems.
- Have basic skill levels in:
  - Monitoring & maintaining critical process parameters.
  - Performing changeover and set-up.
  - Reduction of minor stoppages and adjustments.
- Record / Collect data to track equipment performance:
  - Production control chart.
  - Work order system.

The Maintenance Role

- Provide technical support and training.
- Restore deteriorated equipment.
- Identify design weaknesses and improve the equipment.
- Improve technical maintenance skills of all maintenance personnel.
- Implement planned or periodic maintenance system.
- Perform appropriate maintenance to avoid equipment failure.

I
Autonomous Maintenance

Autonomous Maintenance

The term 'Autonomous Maintenance' is coined by the Japan Institute of Plant Maintenance to describe the shift towards the machine operators maintaining their own equipment.

7 Steps to Autonomous Maintenance

- **Step 1:** Initial cleanup - **7S** campaign.
- **Step 2:** Identify and eliminate root cause of machine stoppages.
- **Step 3:** Establish data collection and standards.
- **Step 4:** Develop standard operating conditions.
- **Step 5:** Train work-cell associates on equipment functions.
- **Step 6:** Identify spare parts and tools required and availability.
- **Step 7:** Improve and measure results.

Step 1
Initial Clean-up
(outside the machine)

- Closely aligned with '**7S**'.
- Clean and clear.
- Identify & tag sources of defects / waste.

The '7S' System

1S	**Separate**	Separate and eliminate any unnecessary items.
2S	**Straighten**	Put all items in order for easy access & cleaning.
3S	**Scrub**	Clean tools, equipment and the workplace.
4S	**Safety**	Ensure that all safety devices are in place.
5S	**Spread**	Make the cleaning & checking in steps 1-4, a habit in the workplace.
6S	**Standardize**	Standardize the previous 5 steps throughout the organization.
7S	**Satisfy**	Satisfy the internal & external customers.

Step 2
Eliminate Root Causes of Defects
(outside the machine)

- Apply the **'5 Whys'.**
- Replace cracked parts.
- Replace worn out parts.
- Set-up workshops.
- Modify equipment for easier checking.

Step 3
Establish Data Collection and Standards

- **Create standards for clean-up and checking:**
  - What equipment should be cleaned and checked?
  - How to properly clean & check the equipment?
  - What points should be checked?
  - Who should check?
  - What check sheet should be used?
  - How to react to changes?
- **Establish standards for data collection:**
  - Production Control Chart

Step 4
Develop Standard Operating Conditions

- Develop methods & standards to routinely verify key process parameters – 'Standard Operating Conditions'.
- Operator executes routine verification & adjustments if necessary.

Step 5
Train People on Equipment Functions

- Operators and team leaders trained to understand the basics of the equipment:
  - Hydraulics
  - Air pressure
  - Electrical / Electronics
  - Lubrication
  - Mechanical
- Engineers, supervisors and operators:
  - Tear down equipment
  - Analyze defects
  - Present findings to the steering committee

Step 6
Identify Spare Parts & Tools Orderliness

- **Improve on supply activity:**
  - Spare parts suppliers leveraged.
  - Spare parts stores at point of use.
  - Spare parts inventory on MRP.

- **Improve on tool availability:**
  - Tool orderliness.
  - Frequently used tools and parts at work station.
  - Make it visible. Apply visual controls.

Step 7
Measure Results and Improve

Monitor TPM Progress with Key Measurables

- Planned vs. Emergency Work.
- Mean Time Between Failure (MTBF).
- Mean Time To Repair (MTTR).
- Quick Change Time Reduction.
- Production Control Charts.
- Zero Lost Time Accidents.
- Scrap Reduction & Zero Defects.

Goals & Objectives of Autonomous Maintenance

- Stabilize, control or prevent deterioration of production equipment.
- Prevent degradation related failures.
- Increase access and ease of inspection and maintenance.
- Improve skill levels & personal growth throughout the organization.
- Improve predictability through data analysis & communication.

II Breakdown Maintenance

Three Steps to "Standardized Breakdown Work"

1. **Identify root cause**
2. **Eliminate cause**
3. **Standardize preventive work to eliminate re-occurrence**

1. Identify Root Cause

- Review Pareto analysis of production down-time.
- Define elements within down-time code causing process stoppages.
- Detailed inspection of machine symptoms.
- Identify root cause elements - use '5 Whys?'.
- Brainstorm & create preliminary action plan.

2. Eliminate Cause

- Replace worn or failing parts.
- Re-calibrate basic operating parameters.
- Eliminate each root cause for the answers to the '5 why questions'.
- Try-out / Validate the repairs.

3. Standardize Work

- Write a detailed description of the repair.
- Specify special techniques or requirements.
- Determine the frequency that repairs need to be made.
- Create maintenance work-order to prevent reoccurrence.
- Include detailed instructions from above in database.

III
Planned Maintenance

Planned Maintenance Objectives

- Reduction of **Mean Time To Repair (MTTR).**
- Increase of **Mean Time Between Failure (MTBF).**
- Less than 1% of maintenance hours for **Reactive Maintenance.**

Planned Maintenance

- **Maximize Mean Time Between Failure (MTBF)**
  - Machine breakdown.
  - Tool breakdown.
  - Performance degradation or part failure.
- **Minimize Mean Time To Repair (MTTR)**
  - Diagnose problem quickly & accurately.
  - Correct problem quickly & accurately.
  - Optimized machine set-up to make good parts.
  - Optimized spare parts location & control.
- **Analyze Data & Key Indicators**
  - Breakdown measurements.
  - Problem solving tools.
  - Vibration analysis tools.

IV
Upstream Maintenance

Maintenance Prevention

New Equipment & Tool Design Considerations:

- Input from breakdown maintenance.
- Input from planned maintenance.
- Life cycle costing.
- Design reviews (operators, supervisors, engineers).
- Maintenance and operations manual preparation:
  - Define 'installation, start-up, and adjustments'
  - Define 'initial de-bug requirements'
  - Identify all safety issues
  - Define 'preventive maintenance standards'

PDCA
Plan-Do-Check-Act

PDCA
Plan-Do-Check-Act

PDCA is a four step process for quality improvement as shown below:

PLAN: In the first step, a plan to effect improvement is developed.

DO: In the second step, the plan is carried out.

CHECK: In the third step, corrections are made to the plan.

ACT: In the last step, action is taken to carry out the plan.

This process is repeated till the original plan is achieved.

PDCA Spiral

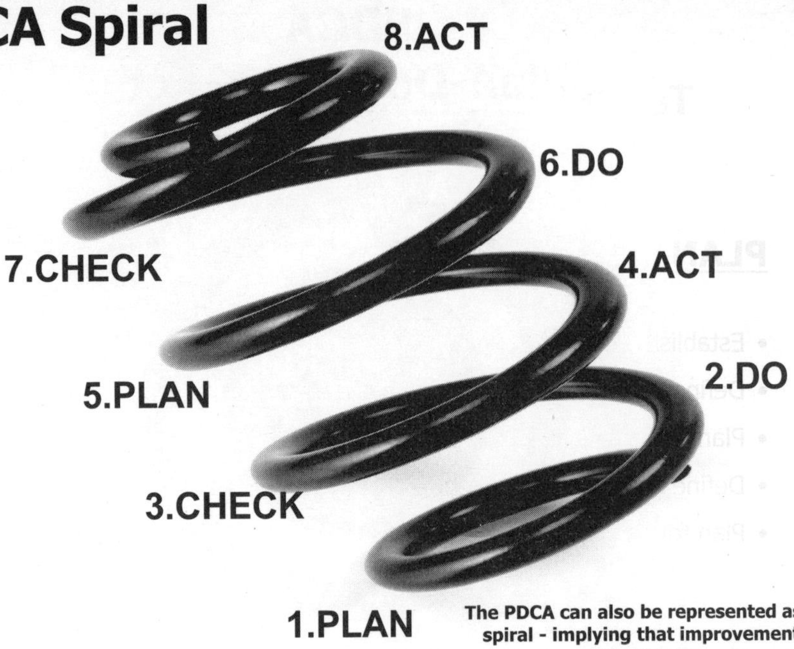
8.ACT
6.DO
7.CHECK
4.ACT
2.DO
5.PLAN
3.CHECK
1.PLAN

The PDCA can also be represented as a spiral - implying that improvement never ceases.

Application of PDCA

Act
Plan
Check
Do

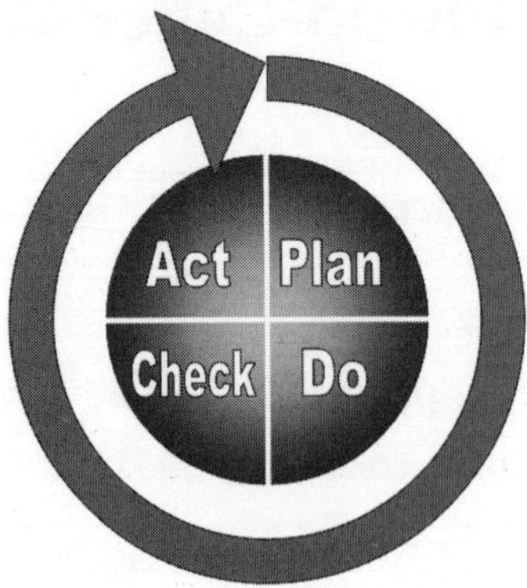

Continual improvement process of Quality Management System can be deployed throughout the organization by undertaking PDCA activities at various levels as shown below.

Top Management

PLAN

- Establish 'Policy'.
- Define 'Objectives'.
- Plan and provide resources.
- Define organization structure.
- Plan for innovating new products.

Top Management...

DO

- Lead by example.
- Show commitment.
- Deploy policy throughout the organization.
- Define measurable objectives.
- Delegate.

Top Management...

CHECK

- Is the system working for us?
- Are we meeting the objectives?
- Is our policy being followed?
- Are our customers happy?
- How is our business doing?
- Are we planning anything that could affect the system?

Top Management...

ACT

- Incorporate review results into strategic planning.
- Provide for additional resources.
- Re-organize.
- Hire new staff.
- Fire non-believers / non-performers.

Department Heads

PLAN

- Establish procedures and instructions for departmental activities.
- Define responsibilities.
- Establish objectives.
- Plan resources including training of personnel.
- Establish communication channel for instructions and feed-back.

Department Heads...

DO

- Allocate clear responsibilities.
- Provide resources and support.
- Co-ordinate and harmonize activities.
- Resolve problems.

Department Heads...

CHECK

- How is the department performing?
- Are the processes under control?
- Are we meeting the internal customer requirements?
- Are we meeting our departmental objectives?
- What are the key problem areas?
- How can we improve?

Department Heads...

ACT

- Develop action plans to meet objectives.
- Focus on improvements.
- Review existing procedures with key measures.
- Provide support and resources.

Management Representative

PLAN

- Co-ordination of key processes, their sequences and interactions.
- Define needs for documented procedures.
- Co-ordinate for preparation of Quality Manual.
- Co-ordinate for elaboration of inter-functional procedures.
- Determine legal and regulatory requirements.
- Co-ordinate Quality Planning.

Management Representative...

DO

- Ensure that the processes are defined & maintained.
- Promote customer focus.
- Facilitate internal communication.
- Support line management functions.
- Co-ordinate training activities.
- Collate measurement data (Product / Process / System).

Management Representative...

CHECK

- Is everyone managing their processes?
- Are the customers happy?
- Is our system working?
- Are we communicating adequately?
- How can we improve?

Management Representative...

ACT

- Stimulate / Co-ordinate inter-functional actions.
- Review internal audit frequency.
- Alert top management.

Application of PDCA

PDCA should be repeatedly implemented, as quickly as possible, in upward **spirals** that converge on the ultimate goal, each cycle closer than the previous one.

This approach is based on the understanding that our knowledge and skills are always limited, but always improving as we go on. PDCA will not only help in defining the ideal goal, it will also help get us in getting there.

Measures of Business Excellence

Excellence Measures

If the performance of any system or process is not measured, it can not be meaningfully and continuously improved. Quantifiable 'Measures of Excellence' for different business functions are as follows:

Marketing

Product strategy

- Sales growth rate.
- Market share.
- Rate of successful new product introductions.

Distribution strategy

- Distribution and sales force productivity.
- Distribution cost per channel.

Marketing...

Others

- Accuracy of forecast assumptions.
- Number of incorrect order entries.
- Overstocked field supplies.
- Contract errors.
- Late deliveries.
- Customer complaints.
- Warranty cost as a percentage of sales.

Purchase

- Premium freight cost / demurrage charges.
- Down-time because of parts shortages.
- Number of off-specification parts used to keep the line going.
- Cycle-time from start of purchase request until items in house.
- Excess inventory.
- Percentage of purchased material rejected on receipt.

Manufacturing

- Yield per ton of raw materials.
- Percentage of parts scrapped.
- Percentage of parts re-worked.
- Percentage of parts accepted on concession.
- Percentage of final product graded as seconds.
- Production per man / machine.
- Percent of production capacity in use.
- Average set-up time.

Product Engineering

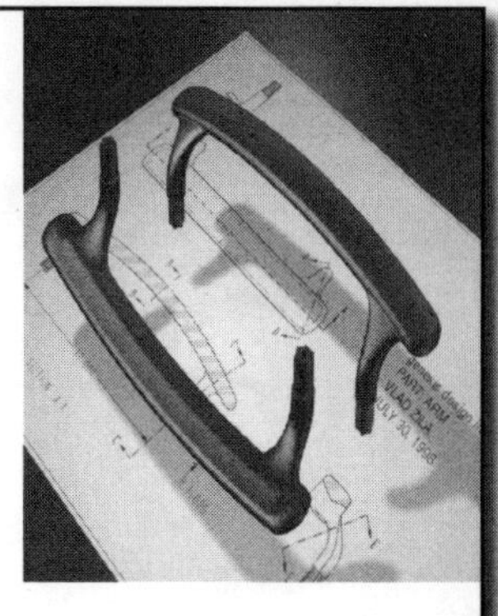

- Number of engineering changes per document.
- Number of errors found during design review.
- Number of errors found in design evaluation test.
- Time over-run compared to planned time for development.
- Percentage of cost over-run over estimated cost of development.
- Number of tooling re-design after trial production.

Quality Assurance

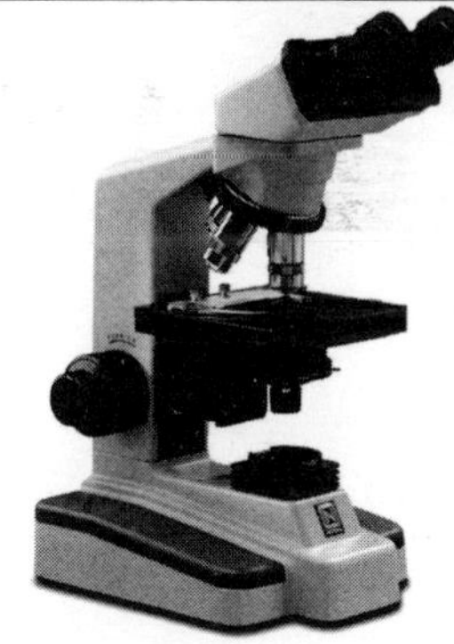

- Percentage of lots rejected due to errors.
- Percentage of products having defects detected by customers.
- Number of engineering changes that should have been detected in design review.
- Errors in inspection / test reports.
- Cycle-time to get corrective actions.
- Percentage of appraisal cost compared to production cost.

Product Reliability

- Mean time to failure.
- Failure rate.
- Probability of failure occurrence during given time interval.
- Probability of failure non-occurrence during given time interval.
- Mean life time.
- Mean time to first generate overhaul.
- Mean time to repair.

Accounting

- Percentage of late payments.
- Time to respond to customers.
- Billing errors.
- Incorrect accounting entries.
- Payroll errors.
- Errors in cost estimates.

Finance

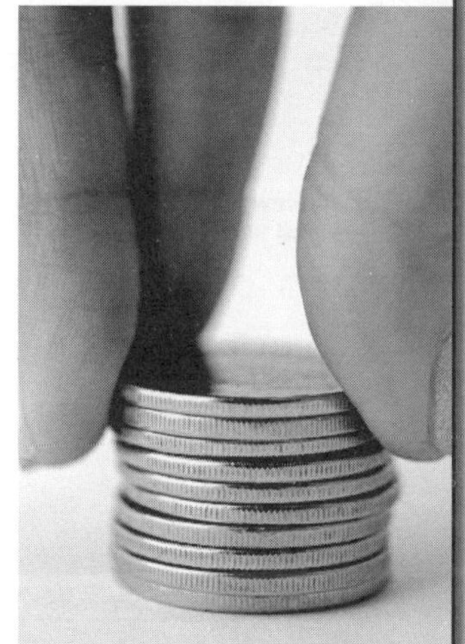

- Cost of quality as a percentage of sales.
- Profit before interest and financial charges.
- Profit before and after tax.
- Growth in profits over last year.
- Return on assets.
- Return on capital employed.
- Return on sales.

Employees

- Sales per employee.
- Offer to acceptance ratio.
- Average employee tenure.
- Internal promotions.
- Employee turnover ratio.
- Suggestions received and implemented.
- Recruitment cost as a percentage of sales.
- Time needed to train the new employees.
- Man-hours lost due to labor problems.

Dynamic Measurement System

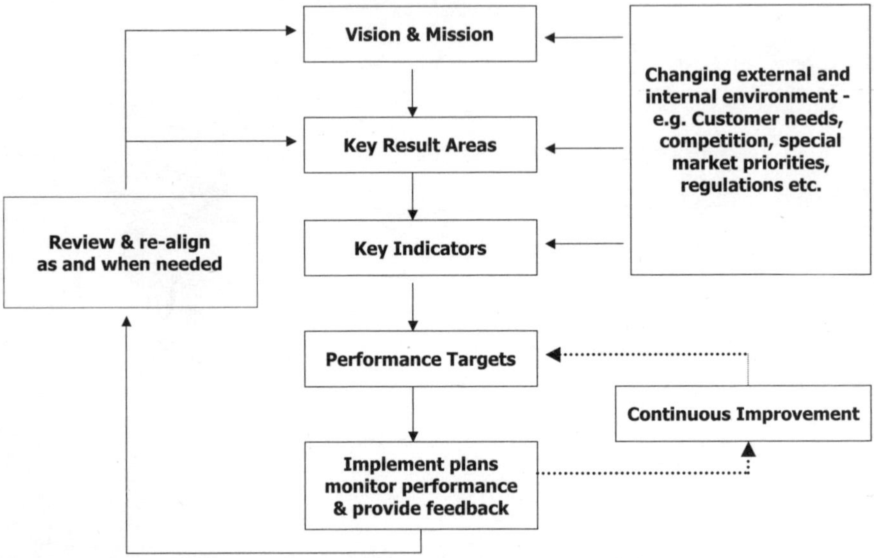

Vision & Mission

Key Result Areas

Key Indicators

Performance Targets

Implement plans monitor performance & provide feedback

Review & re-align as and when needed

Changing external and internal environment - e.g. Customer needs, competition, special market priorities, regulations etc.

Continuous Improvement

The objective is to raise the bar continuously.

6

Quality

"I have offended God and mankind because my work didn't reach the quality it should have."

Leonardo-Da-Vinci
The greatest painter of all times.

**"Quality is never an accident;
it is always the result of high intention,
sincere effort,
intelligent direction and
skillful execution;
it represents the wise choice of many
alternatives,
the cumulative experience of many
masters of craftsmanship.
Quality also marks the search for an ideal
after necessity has been satisfied and
mere usefulness achieved."**

William A. Foster

**"Quality in a product or service is not what
the supplier puts in.
It is what the customer gets out and is
willing to pay for.
A product is not quality because it is hard
to make and costs a lot of money, as
manufacturers typically believe.
Customers pay only for what is of use to
them and gives them value.
Nothing else constitutes quality."**

Peter Drucker

"Quality is a comparative concept, and always will be dynamic. That is why no one has ever reached the optimum. It does not exist and never can."

Hutchins

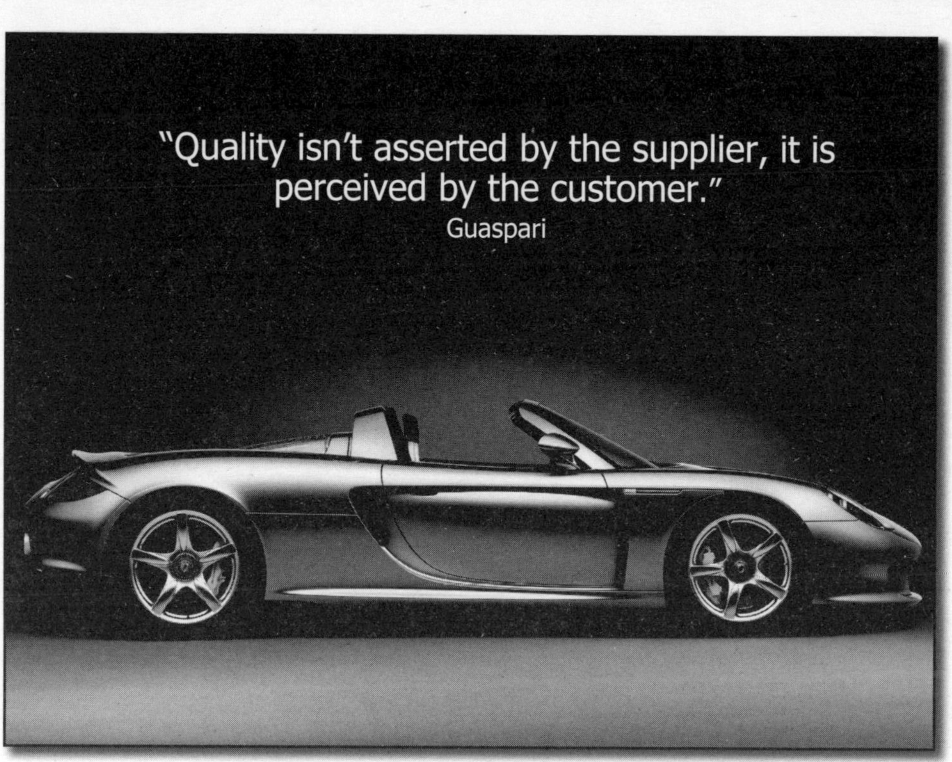

"Quality is meeting or exceeding customer expectations at a cost that represents value to them."

Harrington

"The finest sales talk in the world will not act as a substitute for Quality."

C.G. Campbell

Quality

In technical usage, quality can have two meanings:

- The characteristics of a product or service that bear on its ability to **satisfy stated or implied customer needs.**
- A product or service **free from deficiencies.**

Quality

ISO 9000 : 2000 version defines Quality as:

"Degree to which a set of inherent characteristics fulfills requirements."

Quality can also be expressed by the following formula:

$$\text{Quality} = \frac{\text{Performance}}{\text{Expectations}}$$

Key Components of Product Quality

- Meets needs of the customers
- Performance / Functionality / Features
- Design / Visual impact
- Desirability / Elegance / Emotional appeal
- Attention to fine details
- Affordability / Suitability / Maintainability
- Accessibility / Availability
- Reliability / Durability
- Ease / Free from difficulties
- Speed / Timeliness
- Accuracy
- Security / Dependability / Safety
- Self-esteem / Uniqueness / Exclusivity
- WOW factors / Amazing / Surprise elements

Quality Process Grid

Right Things Wrong	**Wrong Things Right**
Wrong Things Wrong	**Right Things Right** ✓

Quality, Cost & Profit Relationship

Many people think that quality costs money and adversely effects profits.

Quality in the long run results in increased profitability.

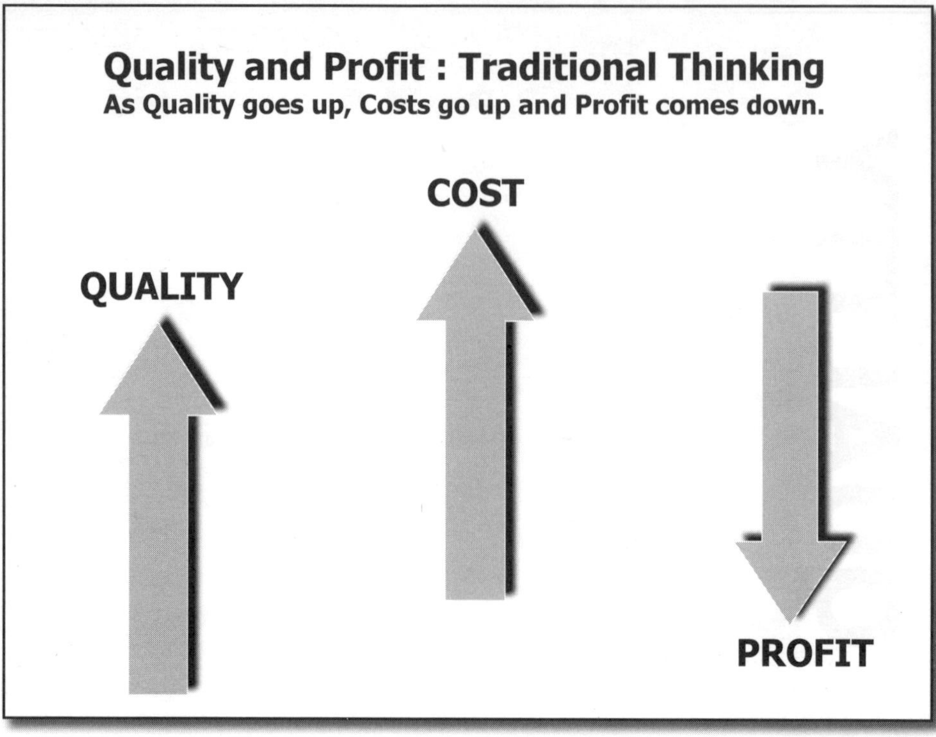
Quality and Profit : Traditional Thinking
As Quality goes up, Costs go up and Profit comes down.
COST
QUALITY
PROFIT

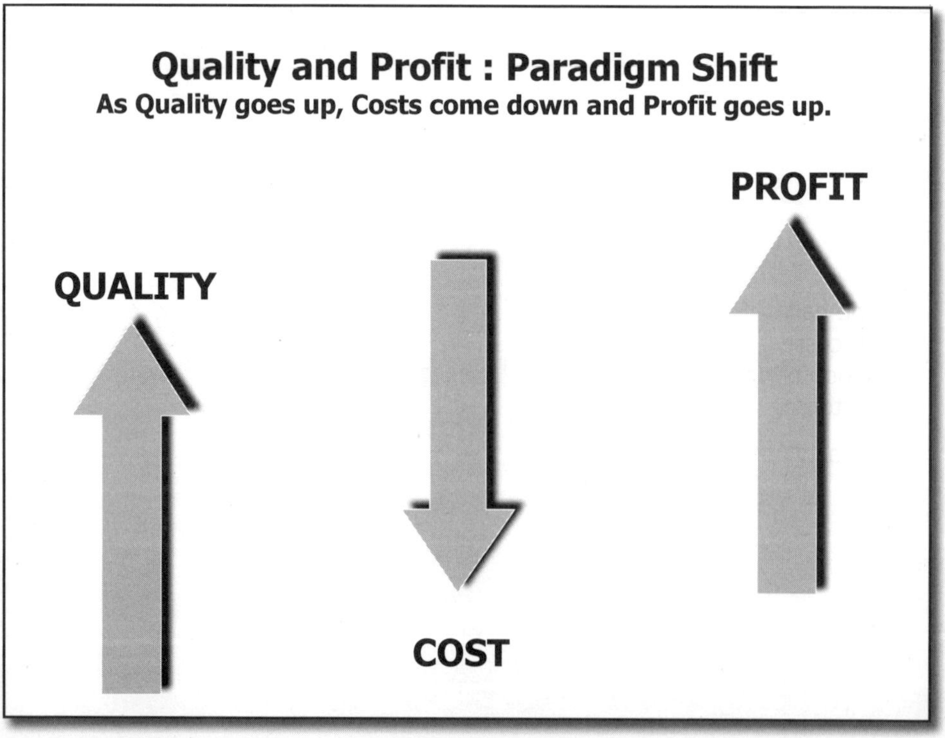
Quality and Profit : Paradigm Shift
As Quality goes up, Costs come down and Profit goes up.
PROFIT
QUALITY
COST

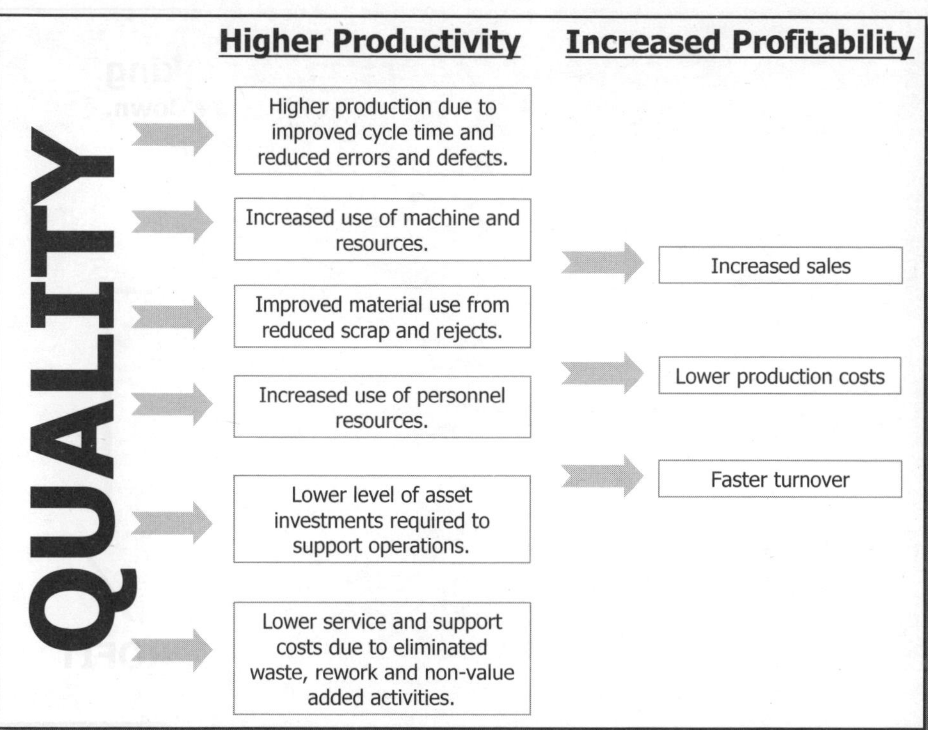

'Quality'
A WIN-WIN Ideology

The hallmarks of quality organizations are high return, high performing processes, empowered, well paid and highly motivated personnel, good corporate citizenship, respect for the environment and delighted customers.

'Quality' – A total ideology, creates an ideal **WIN-WIN** situation for all.

Quality Policy Deployment

Quality Ripple Effect

Quality Policy Deployment is the mechanism by which the quality effort is cascaded down throughout the organization. A well deployed quality policy has a **Ripple effect** in the organization.

Quality Policy Deployment

Quality policy deployment is a mechanism, which is used for deploying corporate goals at all levels in the organization and managing Quality strategically. Quality policy deployment is the translation of Japanese words **'Hoshin Kanri'**. 'Hoshin' means 'direction' and 'Kanri' means 'deployment or administration'.

Quality Policy Deployment...

Quality policy deployment is a key process by which an organization can articulate and communicate the Vision, Mission, Goals and vital few programs to all employees. It provides the answers to the two questions:

- **What do we need to do? and**
- **How are we going to do it?**

Essential Steps

- Issue of 'Corporate Quality Policy' for the year, laying down quantified targets and milestones for monitoring the progress.
- Formulation of sub-policies of different departments and identification of critical processes.
- Interfacing with other departments / functional groups and agreement on inputs required along with the time schedule.

Essential Steps...

- Preparation of departmental plans for identified activities, with well defined targets, methods and allocation of responsibilities down to the lowest operating level.
- Implementation of plan after providing necessary resources including training and requisite information.

Essential Steps...

- Periodic monitoring of policy deployment progress by departments along with co-ordination meetings with other related departments to sort out operational problems in achieving departmental targets.
- Top management reviews at regular intervals to ascertain the progress of policy deployment and taking mid course corrective action for attainment of organizational goals.

Directions for Implementing Quality

Planning

- Gather and review data from customers.
- Gather and review data from employees.
- Gather and review data on processes.
- Develop a plan to achieve short-term Quality goals.
- Develop a plan to achieve long-term Quality objectives.
- Assign accountability for implementing the Quality plan.
- Develop ways to measure the success of the implementation.
- Re-visit the Quality plan to identify changes and document results.

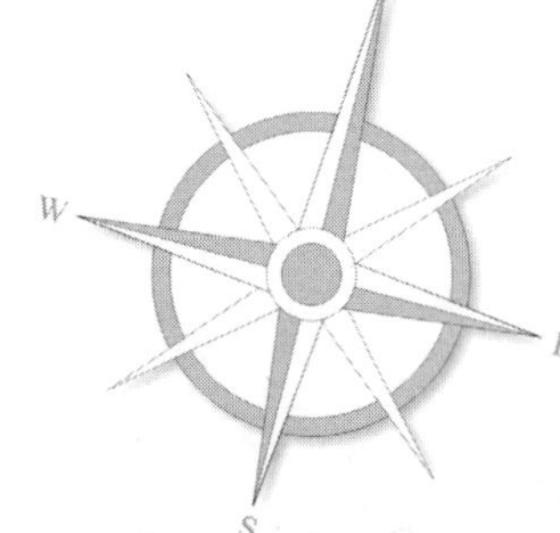

Leadership & Commitment

- Work together as a team to create the organizational mission vision, values and implementation strategies.
- Train others in the organization in Quality.
- Reinforce Quality through rewards, recognition and promotions.
- Maintain close and direct contact with key customers.
- Create an empowering environment.
- Hold managers accountable for implementing Quality.
- Take ownership for key process improvements.

Infrastructure

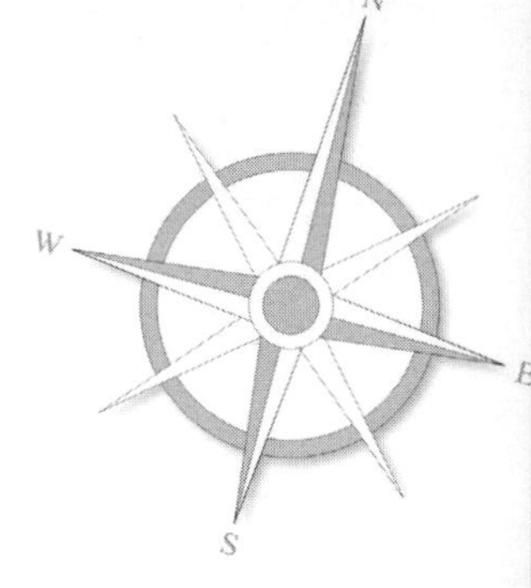

- Develop a Quality infrastructure.
- Identify, train and empower internal Quality champions.
- Develop a process for monitoring Quality.
- Identify, select and train individuals to consult internally on Quality implementation.
- Designate one person to be directly accountable to the senior most person to execute implementation details.

Focus & Rollout

- Develop a Quality rollout.
- Target short-term goals & the key processes to improve.
- Identify the key managers who will implement Quality.
- Identify key locations for implementing Quality.

Focus & Rollout...

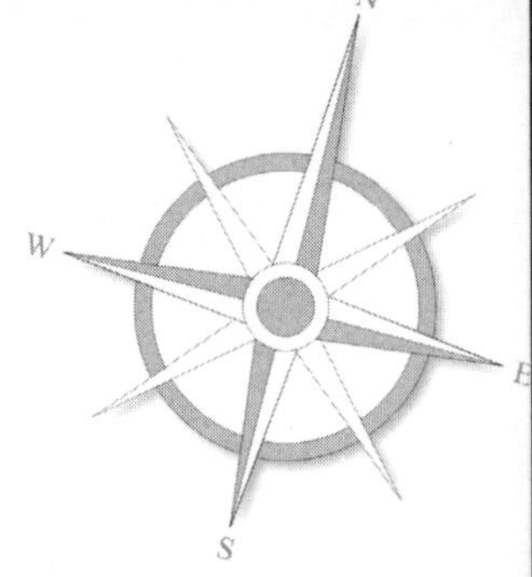

- Target the customer priorities.
- Target key processes for improvement and assign responsibilities for improving them with time frame.
- Set stretch objectives for improvement along critical lines like cost, time and delivery for each targeted process.
- Target long-term needs for more complex processes.

Measurement

- Review existing measures in the light of Quality priorities.
- Develop Quality measurement strategy and plan.
- Develop customer-driven listening strategies and measures.
- Establish measures to track employee satisfaction.
- Establish new measures to track process improvement.

Measurement...

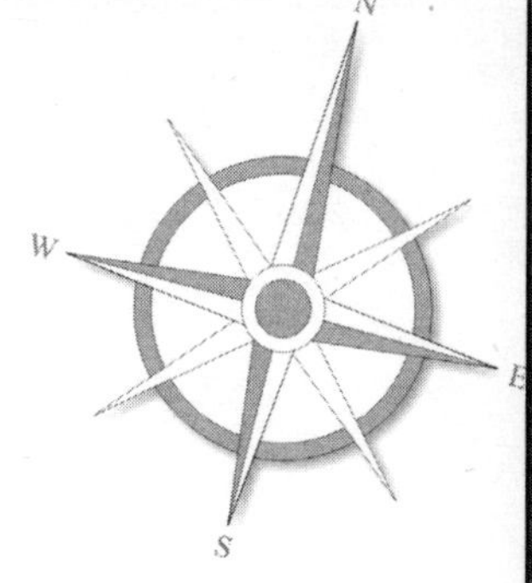

- Establish measures to track organizational improvement.
- Develop measurement tracking and reporting systems.
- Benchmark with world-class organizations.

Training

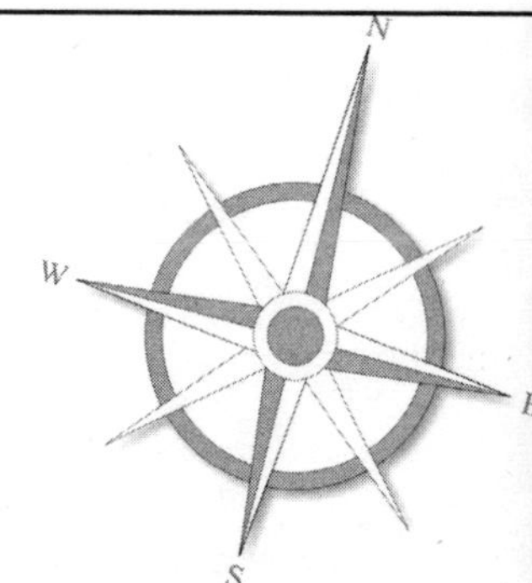

- Develop Quality training strategy and plan.
- Identify gaps between current training and Quality training needs.
- Identify training sources to develop and deliver training.
- Allocate resources.
- Identify and train the best people to be facilitators.
- Develop measures of training effectiveness that reflect feedback from customers, employees and processes.

Resources

- Identify and fulfill Quality needs for financial support.
- Consider the needs of the customer when allocating resources.
- Incorporate Quality into annual planning and budgeting processes.
- Consider commitments to suppliers when allocating resources.

Information & Communication

- Gather and integrate information critical to Quality implementation.
- Assign a senior process-owner to manage information and communication.
- Develop a Quality communication strategy and plan, focussing on employees.
- Communicate a personal statement from the CEO about commitment to Quality.
- Provide systematic and periodic updates to your customers and suppliers.

Systems

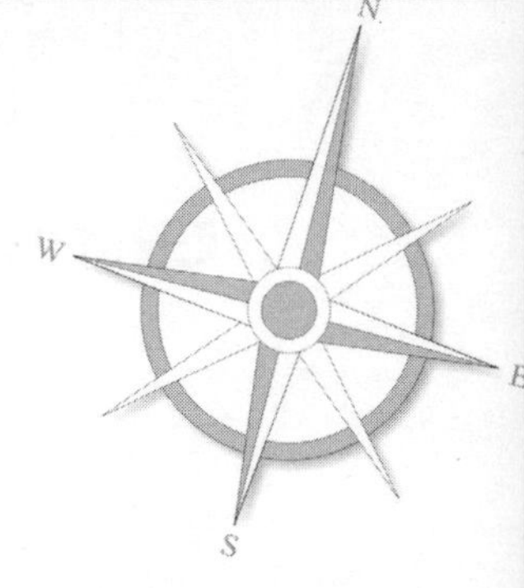

- Align Quality with strategic planning.
- Align Quality with other key organizational processes.
- Align Quality with customer needs.
- Include Quality improvement in every person's job description.

Customers

- Identify key customers.
- Develop a customer alignment strategy and plan.
- Establish valid customer requirements and expectations.
- Develop and use customer satisfaction measures.
- Create partner relationships with key customers.
- Link customer requirements to the development of new products and services.

Customers...

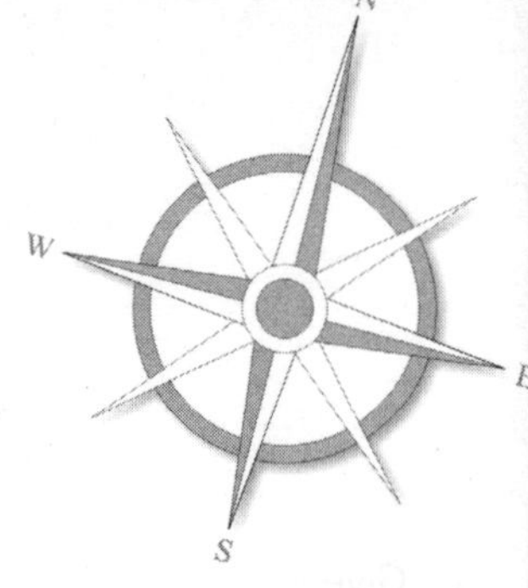

- Develop and communicate policies.
- Empower everyone in the organization to serve the customers.
- Anticipate future needs of the customers.
- Benchmark with key competitors to analyze gaps and make improvements.
- Gather continuous feedback from customers.

Suppliers

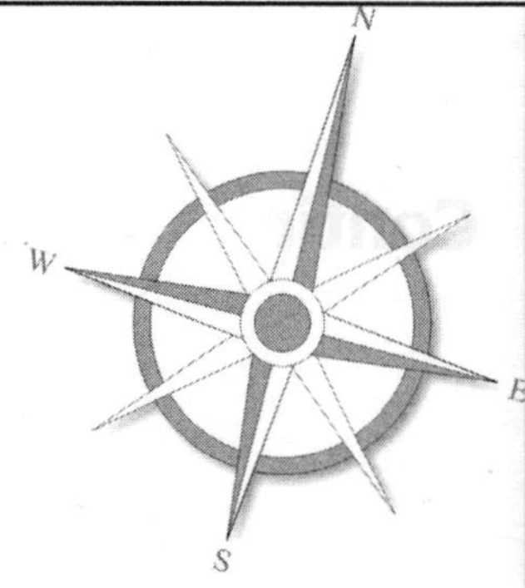

- Identify key suppliers.
- Develop a supplier alignment strategy and pan.
- Establish valid supplier requirements and expectations.
- Develop and use supplier satisfaction measures.
- Use a vendor certification process.
- Create partner relationships with key suppliers.
- Anticipate the future requirements of suppliers.

Suppliers...

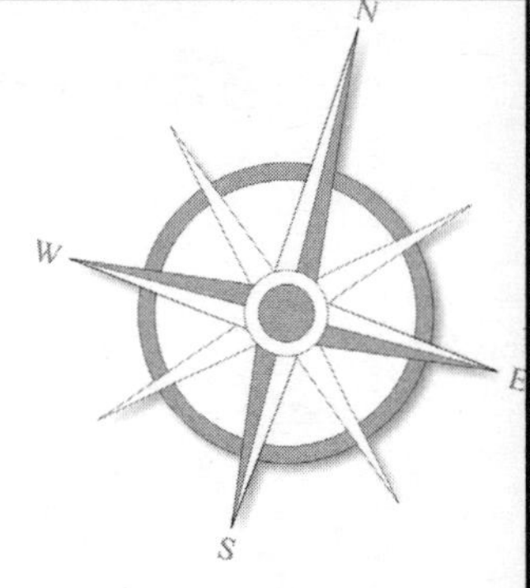

- Give supplier awards.
- Offer TQM training to suppliers.
- Benchmark with key suppliers to learn how competitors are operating.
- Gather continuous feedback from suppliers.
- Empower everyone in the organization to improve relationships with suppliers.

Continuous Improvement

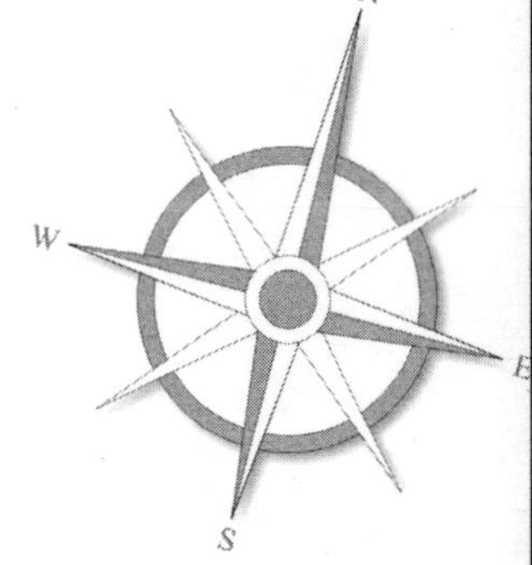

- Continuously improve key performance measures.*
- Do regular PDCA - Plan, Do, Check & Act.

*** Refer section 5 – 'Excellence measures' for more details.**

Three Approaches to Quality

Materialistic Approach

- In the materialistic approach, the organization is only concerned about the ultimate business results and does not focus on systems and people involvement.
- They skip important steps and treat people as mechanical beings. These kind of organizations usually end up in a chaotic situation.

Ritualistic Approach

- The organizations go after systematic approach without adequate focus on people involvement and results.
- They end up simply creating beaurocracy and the results do not show any improvement.
- People lose faith and confidence. Following systems and procedures is no guarantee of quality.

Spiritualistic Approach

Under this approach, the organizations focus completely on people involvement and create lot of enthusiasm. They, however, fail to channelize people's energy through proper systems and well defined approaches towards the end results - Thus, even these organizations end up without much success.

Balancing Act

Successful implementation of **Quality** requires the balancing act between all the three approaches without over or under doing any one aspect.

Reducing Quality Costs

Categories of Quality Costs

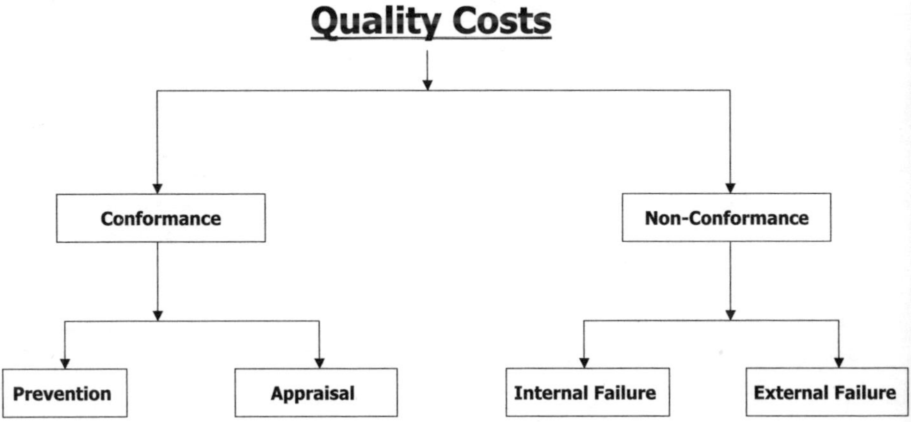

Quality Costs

- **Conformance**
  - **Prevention**
  - **Appraisal**
- **Non-Conformance**
  - **Internal Failure**
  - **External Failure**

Cost of Quality

- **Cost of quality = Cost of conformance + Cost of non-conformance**
- Cost of conformance is the cost of providing 'products or services as per the required standards.' This can be termed as **good amount spent**. (Prevention & Appraisal costs)
- Cost of non-conformance is the failure cost associated with a 'process not being operated to the requirements'. This can be termed as **unnecessary amount spent**. (Internal & External failure costs)

Cost Management Vs. Cost Cutting

Most of the organizations have wrong notions about cost. They confuse quality cost management with cost cutting measures.

It is extremely important to understand that cost management is different from cost cutting. Cutting the conformance costs in the form of prevention or appraisal costs, will actually increase the costs in the long run.

Visible and Hidden Costs

It is important to know that visible quality costs are merely the tip of the ice-berg. Organizations should focus their attention in controlling the hidden quality costs, which form the substantial portion of the total quality costs. These costs do not get controlled as they are not appropriately reflected by the financial accounting systems.

Visible Costs are 'Tip of the Ice-berg'

Visible costs

- Scrap
- Re-work
- Warranty costs

Hidden Costs

- Conversion efficiency of materials
- Inadequate resource utilization
- Excessive use of material
- Cost of re-design and re-inspection
- Cost of resolving customer problems
- Lost customers / Goodwill
- High inventory

Prevention Costs

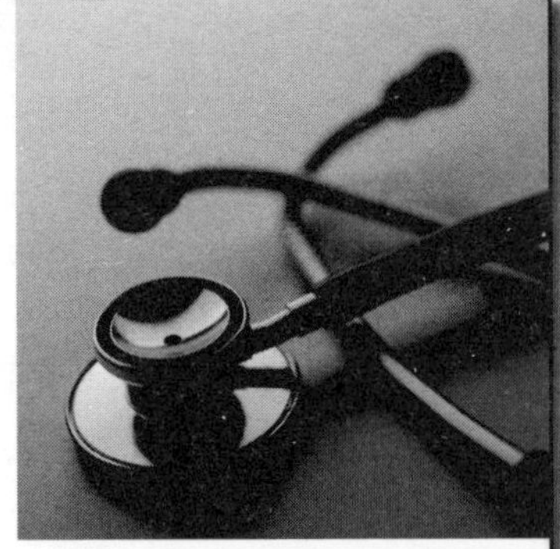

- Prevention costs are associated with design, implementation, maintenance and planning prior to actual operation, in order to avoid defects from happening.
- The emphasis on the prevention activities reduces the probability of producing the defective products. Prevention activities lead to reduction of appraisal costs and both type of failure costs (internal and external).
- The motto is **"Prevention rather than appraisal".**

Activities Associated with Prevention Costs

- Market research.
- Quality training programs.
- Contract review.
- Design review.
- Field trials.
- Supplier evaluation.
- Process plan review.
- Process capability review.
- Design of jigs and fixtures.
- Preventive maintenance.

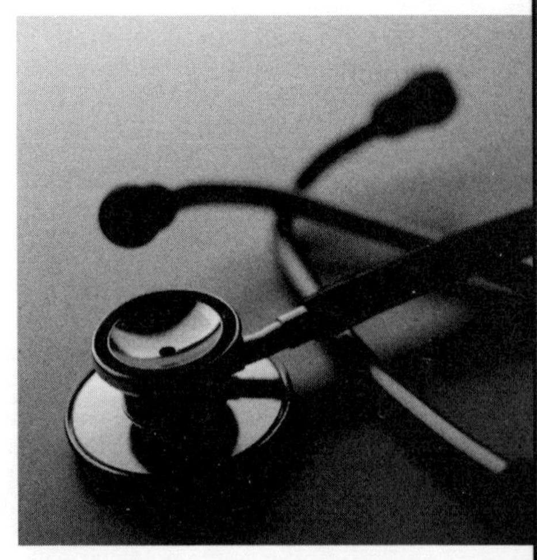

Appraisal Costs

Appraisal costs are spent to detect the defects to ensure conformance to the required quality standards. Appraisal costs are associated with "cost of checking if things are correct". The appraisal costs are focused on the discovery of defects rather than prevention of defects.

Activities Associated with Appraisal Costs

- Prototype testing.
- Vendor surveillance.
- Incoming material inspection.
- Process inspection / control.
- Final inspection.
- Laboratory testing / measurement.
- Depreciation cost for measuring.
- Quality audits.

Internal Failure Costs

Internal failure costs occur when the results of a work fail to reach the designated quality standards and are detected before the products are transferred to the customers.

Activities Associated with Internal Failure Costs

- Design changes / corrective action.
- Scrap due to design changes.
- Excess inventory.
- Rectification / reject disposition of purchased material.
- Re-work / rejection in manufacturing.
- Down-grading of end product.
- Down-time of plant & machinery.
- Trouble-shooting & investigation of defects.

External Failure Costs

External failure costs occur when the product or service from a process fails to reach the designated quality standards and is not detected until it is **transferred to the customer.**

Activities Associated with External Failure Costs

- Investigation of customer complaints.
- Repair / Replacement of sold goods.
- Warranty claims.
- Product liability & litigation costs.
- Interest charges on delayed payment due to quality problems.
- Loss of customer goodwill & sales.

Size of Various Quality Costs

- In many organizations, there is less emphasis on prevention and their main quality efforts are focused on appraisal activities, with very little control on internal and external failure costs.
- Various studies have shown that quality costs in manufacturing organizations range from 20% to 30% of turnover.

Less Emphasis on Prevention Cost Leads to Rise in Quality Costs.

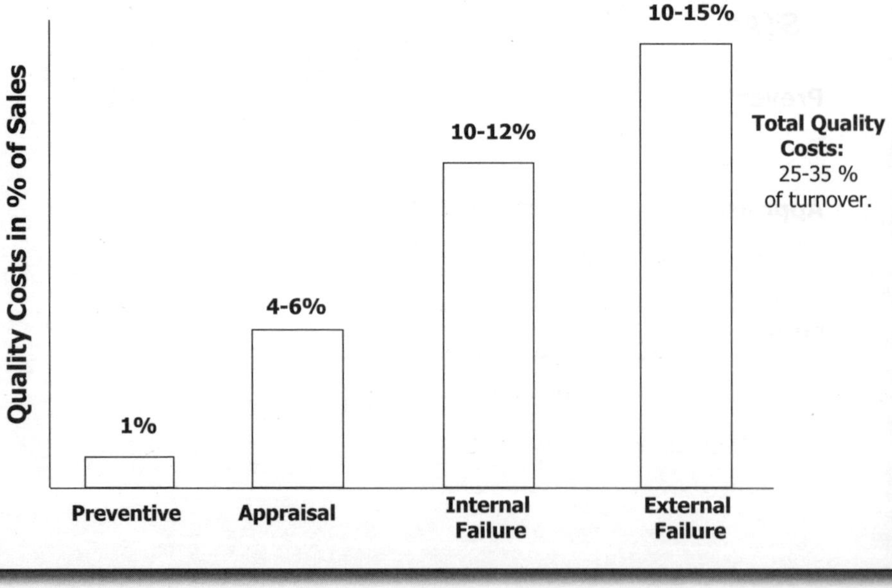

Category	Quality Costs in % of Sales
Preventive	1%
Appraisal	4-6%
Internal Failure	10-12%
External Failure	10-15%

Total Quality Costs: 25-35 % of turnover.

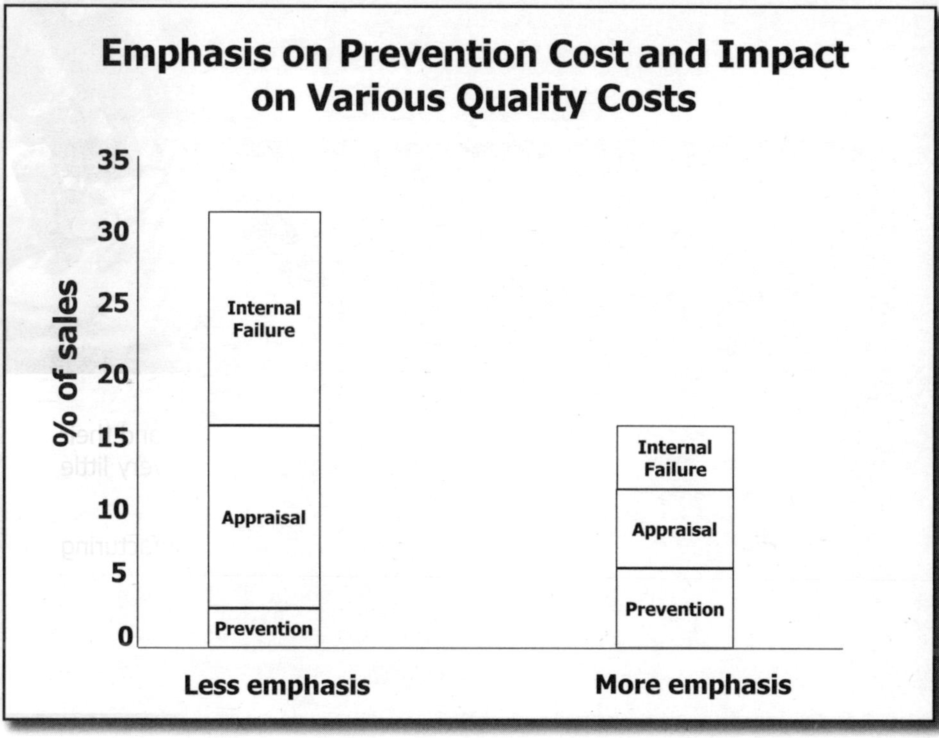
Emphasis on Prevention Cost and Impact on Various Quality Costs
% of sales
35
30
25
20
15
10
5
0
Internal Failure
Appraisal
Prevention
Internal Failure
Appraisal
Prevention
Less emphasis
More emphasis

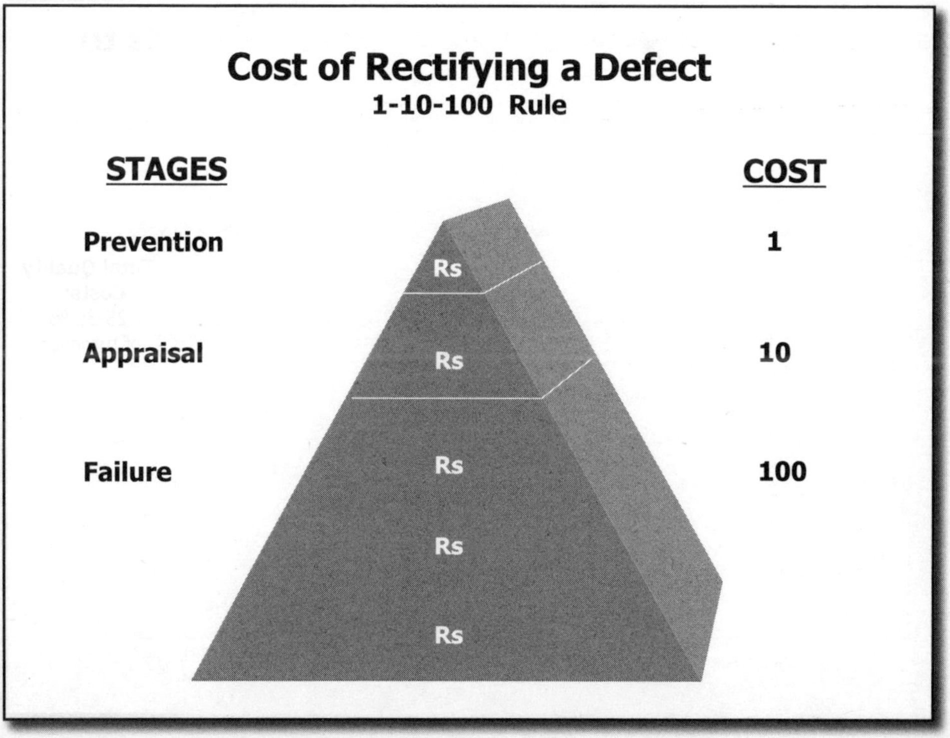
Cost of Rectifying a Defect
1-10-100 Rule
STAGES
COST
Prevention
1
Appraisal
10
Failure
100
Rs
Rs
Rs
Rs
Rs

Function Wise Analysis of Quality Costs

Quality Assurance

Prevention Costs	Appraisal Costs	Failure Costs
• Quality planning. • Training personnel.	• Process appraisal. • Final product appraisal.	• Internal failure. • External failure.

Research, Design and Development

Prevention Costs	Appraisal Costs	Failure Costs
• Setting specifications of services, materials, processes and products. • Pre-production / operation and prototype trials.	• Inspection of equipments: - Maintenance - Design & specifications	• Re-work & rectification. • Down-grading of products & services. • Product or service complaints & warranty claims.

Production / Operations

Prevention Costs	Appraisal Costs	Failure Costs
• Training - including supervisor training. • Pre-production / operation and prototype trials. • Special handling & storage during production or operations. • Supervision of quality at all stages.	• Line or process inspection by production & operations personnel. • Finished product inspection or service checking by production & operations personnel.	• Full cost of scrap or wasted effort. • Re-work & rectification. • Replacement of rejected product or repeating service. • Down-grading of products, materials and services.

Marketing and Sales

Prevention Costs	Appraisal Costs	Failure Costs
• Market research. • Correct forecasts. • Setting of correct product or service specifications as per the requirement of customers.	• Analysis of degree of acceptance of goods and services.	• Down-grading of products and services. • Customer complaints, liaison & compensation. • Warranty claims & replacements or refunds.

Purchasing

Prevention Costs	Appraisal Costs	Failure Costs
• Supplier evaluation. • Supplier training.	• Vendor rating. • Receiving inspection.	• Down-time because of part shortages.

Service Department

Prevention Costs	Appraisal Costs	Failure Costs
• Product or service specification evaluation. • Pre-production, operations and prototype trials. • Planning of in-process control procedures.	• Finished product or service performance evaluation.	• Customer complaints. • Product or customer service. • Returned material investigations and repairs.

Personnel

Prevention Costs	Appraisal Costs	Failure Costs
• Recruitment of appropriate personnel. • Good compensation. • Competencies analysis. • Training.	• Operation of staff appraisal systems.	• Dealing with results of poor recruitment process. • Disciplinary procedures. • Strikes / Union problems. • High employee turnover.

Stores, Transport and Distribution

Prevention Costs	Appraisal Costs	Failure Costs
• Special handling and storage.	• Receiving and checking materials bought-out items or services. • Checking and despatching finished product and services.	• Sorting of reject finished goods in stock. • Receiving and checking returned & rejected goods. • Checking and despatching replacement goods.

Materials Control

Prevention Costs	Appraisal Costs	Failure Costs
• Ordering correct materials. • Inventory systems.	• Checking stock levels.	• Excess inventory. • Scrap material control. • Replacement of material.

Maintenance

Prevention Costs	Appraisal Costs	Failure Costs
• Prototype processes and equipment. • Planning and maintenance of plant equipment and inspection equipment.	• Equipment reliability monitoring.	• Down-time of plant & machinery. • Trouble-shooting and investigation of defects.

Finance

Prevention Costs	Appraisal Costs	Failure Costs
• Establishment of good financial systems with proper controls in place. • Proper assessment of customers on credit facility. • Feasibility studies.	• Auditing accounts. • Determination of quality related costs.	• Investigations following failure in the system. • Chasing recoveries from the customers. • Bad debts. • Losses.

Supplier Quality Improvement

Objectives

- Products are 100% correct & reliable.
- Deliveries are always on time.
- Quantities delivered are always correct.
- Deliveries occur frequently to minimize stock carried by user.
- The supplier provides appropriate response to urgent requirements.
- Total commitment to rectification of mistakes.

Objectives...

- Product pricing is competitive.
- Invoices and documentation are free from errors.
- The supplier is totally open and honest about the processes, costs and pricing methods.
- The supplier works with the company to continuously improve performance.

1. Quality History

- How many lots were received with this part number?
- What % of lots were rejected with this part number?
- What types of defects were identified in receiving inspection note?
- Were the previously committed corrective actions effective?

2. Delivery History

- What % of lots were on time for this part number?
- How many days early or late, the lots are received for this part number?
- Were the previously committed recovery plans effective in improving the delivery?

3. Part / Assembly Drawings and Artwork

- Are all the drawings available?
- Are all drawings complete, signed, dated and released through document control?
- Does the drawing include the latest revision?
- Is the bill of material complete and accurate?
- Are the dimensions and tolerances excessively tight for normal processing and will the special processing be required?

Drawings and Artwork...

- Are there drawing notes, dimensions, tolerances, representing areas where the supplier does not currently have manufacturing experience?
- Does the artwork meet all parameters as called out in the manufacturing specification and fabrication drawing?
- Does the supplier have recommendations to improve the clarity of the drawings?

4. Product Specifications

- Are all the specifications available?
- Are the specifications complete, signed, dated and released?
- Are the specification changes required to support tooling and processes?
- Are there any specifications that exceed the supplier's current technology?

Product Specifications...

- Does the supplier have any difficulty in meeting the specifications?
- Has the engineering dept. completed design verification testing?
- Has regulatory testing been completed and have regulatory approvals been obtained?
- Has reliability and environmental testing been completed?
- Are there recommendations for design changes that will improve product reliability?

5. Cost

- Does the design meet target costs for manufacturing, capital and maintenance?
- Are there recommendations for design changes that will reduce cost?

6. Process

- Is the design capable of being manufactured with the supplier's current process?
- Are there any special equipments required?
- Is the process capable of making the part as designed?
- Are the manufacturing methods documented?
- Does the supplier need assistance in developing the process?
- Are the material handling procedures adequate to prevent damage to the part?

7. Inspection

- Is the drawing clear and understandable?
- Are the materials, finish and form adequately called out?
- Are the standard measuring tools calibrated?
- Are the calibration procedures documented?

Inspection...

- Are the inspection instructions available for each part number? Are they comprehensive?
- Has an inspection study been performed? Are the results of the study acceptable?
- What are the current sampling plans?

Inspection...

- Does the supplier need assistance in developing an inspection plan?
- Does the supplier have a quality management system?
- Is source inspection required at the plant location?
- Is the source inspector trained?

8. Packaging Requirements

- Is shipping protection against moisture / humidity required?
- Is there a special finish on the product that requires special handling?
- Are there special aging and shelf-life limitations?
- Is there a delicate nature to the product which requires special packaging to allow for handling in-house?
- Will the product require special packaging and shipping due to size, weight, mounting or cooling?

9. Manufacturing Schedule

- What is the projected annual volume?
- What is the projected daily volume?
- When is the product scheduled to start production?
- Is the supplier's process capable of manufacturing the required volume and meeting the delivery schedule?

10. Procurement Administration

- Verbal instructions are unacceptable and changes must be backed up by the documentation, including approved marked drawings. Is this procedure being followed internally and with the supplier?
- Are change orders incorporated only after receipt of documentation and in acceptable time by the supplier?
- Are the requirements for the first article specified in the purchase documents?

Procurement Administration...

- Have the quality assurance policies and requirements been included in the purchase documents?
- Has the first article been received, inspected and approved?
- Is the supplier on the approved manufacturers list?
- Are the suppliers aware of the deviations and are they given the opportunity to submit deviation requests prior to shipment of the products?

Audit of Quality Management Systems

Quality Policy

- Has the organization defined its mission?
- Have the factors critical to the accomplishment of mission been analyzed to determine subjects to be controlled by the organization?
- How and by whom has the quality policy been formulated?
- Have the people responsible for implementation been involved in development of the policy?
- How is the quality policy communicated throughout the organization?

Quality Objectives

- Have the quality objectives been defined in measurable terms?
- What is the basis for establishing the quality objectives?
- Have the persons responsible for achieving the objectives been involved in the establishment of quality objectives, in order to secure their commitment?

Quality Objectives...

- How have the risks for achieving the objectives been evaluated?
- Have appropriate objectives been established in different functional areas, which contribute to overall objectives?
- How is the achievement of quality targets verified?
- What analysis is carried out in case of discrepancies between planned and actual results?

Organization

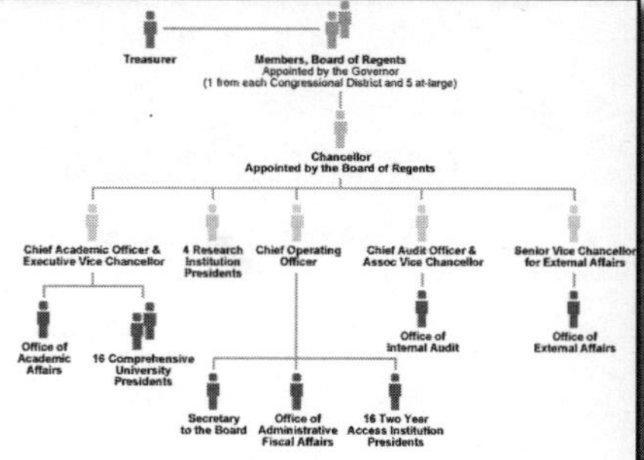

- Is there a well defined organizational structure with clearly defined responsibility and authority at all levels?
- What is the role of the Management Representative and what is the co-ordination process for ensuring that Quality Management System is implemented and maintained in all the functional areas?

Organization...

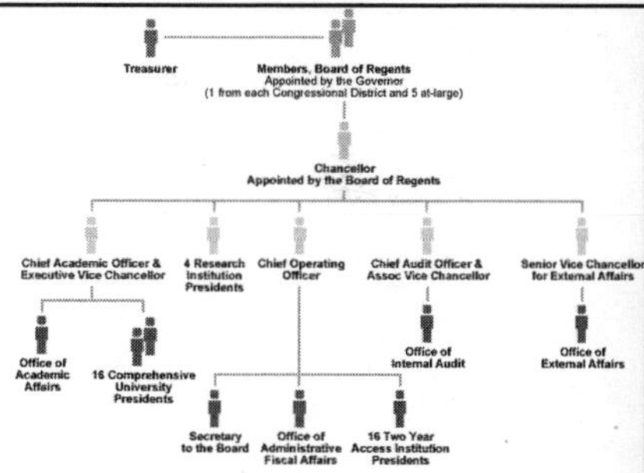

- Does the Management Representative (MR) have appropriate status and authority to effectively co-ordinate the activities of Quality Management Systems throughout the organization?
- How does the MR promote awareness of customer requirements throughout the organization?
- Does the MR have adequate top management support for the satisfactory discharge of his duties?

Human Resource Management

- How are the responsibilities within each role defined and assigned to the various functionaries in the organizational structures?
- How is the need for additional personnel, their qualification and expertise determined?
- How does the recruitment and selection process ensure that the defined requirements of the employees are met?
- What is the process of identifying training and development needs for various employees?

Human Resource Management...

- What is the process for carrying out skills assessment? Does it take into consideration the present job requirements and future business objectives?
- Does the system of appraisal compare the actual performance of the employees with their Key Result Areas (KRAs)?
- How is it ensured that the compensation package is competitive and comparable to the industry standards?
- Is there a transparent and objective system of growth and career progression?

Physical Resource Management

Provision of Resources

- What is the process for provision of physical resources like buildings, utilities, process equipments and supporting services?
- Have the responsibilities for planning and provision of different types of physical resources been defined?
- Has the requirement for any specific work environment that affects conformity to product requirement been identified?

Maintenance of Physical Resources

- Have the processes for maintenance of various types of resources such as buildings and equipment been defined?
- Have the standards of various types of resources been established?
- How are equipment maintenance processes controlled?

Management of Services

- What are the various kinds of services required by the organization? (For example: transportation, cleaning, communication, security, customer service, call center jobs or any other services outsourced.)
- Have the processes for planning, procurement and control of these services been defined and responsibilities allocated?
- Have the key deliverables for these services been established?
- How is the service assessed for conformity and improvement?

Product Realization

- What is the main purpose or output of the process?
- How does the process take the key customer requirements into consideration?
- What information and resources are required for the process?
- What are the key inputs of the process?
- What is the control on the quality of inputs?

Product Realization...

- What are the main stages of the process and how is inter-connection between stages managed?
- What controls are exercised for satisfactory operation of the processes?
- What are the outputs of the process and how are the results of the process measured?
- What action is taken when a desired output is not achieved?
- How are the processes optimized for better yield and throughput?

Marketing Processes

- What market research has been carried out to understand the gaps in demand and supply?
- What are the key factors necessary for the organization to succeed in the market? These factors could be pricing, features, services, quality, ease of operations, accessibility etc.
- How are the present and future needs and expectations of the customers determined?
- Does the marketing strategy take into consideration a proper assessment of competition and external environment?
- How are the customer requirements communicated?

Sales Processes

- Does the sales strategy focus on product, price, promotion and place? What are the sales objectives?
- What are the key stages in the process to achieve the sales objectives?
- How is the information on the organization's products and services conveyed to the potential customers?
- What are the principal activities of the process by which the customer enquiries are converted into orders?

Sales Processes...

- How is the organization's capability to satisfy the customers' requirements determined before accepting the orders?
- How is the customer's requirements conveyed to those who are responsible for their implementation?
- How are the changes in orders / contracts captured, accepted and conveyed to those responsible for their implementation?

Sales Processes...

- What checks are carried out to verify that the customers receive the products and services they have ordered?
- What analysis has been performed to determine the cause in the case of differences between actual and planned results?
- What improvement in results were obtained from the last review of the sales process?

Design & Development Processes

- Is there a proper system for design plan before starting any design and development activity?
- Does the plan identify various design inputs and how these are to be obtained?
- Have the various stages in the design development processes, sequential and parallel work schedules and persons responsible for the completion of design elements been properly defined?
- Has the design and development output been defined in verifiable terms?

Design & Development Processes...

- Is the systematic review of design and development carried out at suitable stages? Is a checklist for such a review available?
- What is the process of design verification? Are the results of verification recorded?
- Is there a design and development validation process, where the resulting product's capability of meeting the requirements of the intended user is demonstrated?
- What is the process of making changes to the design? Are these changes verified and reviewed by the authorized persons before implementation?

Purchase Processes

- Has the organization formulated a purchase policy and relevant guidelines?
- How and by whom are the items to be purchased determined?
- Are the specifications or detailed particulars of all the items to be purchased available?
- What is the process for determining quantities to be purchased?
- How are the legal requirements impacting the purchase of various products determined?

Purchase Processes...

- How are those people who require any products involved in the purchase process?
- How are the suppliers assessed for their ability to supply conforming products?
- Is there an updated list of approved suppliers?
- How is it ensured that the complete information about product specifications is provided to the suppliers?

Purchase Processes...

- What is the process for verifying the qualification of personnel when their skill is critical for ensuring the product quality?
- What is the verification process for critical materials or processes used by any supplier?
- What action is taken when there are minor deviations from the specifications that do not affect the serviceability of the product?
- What actions are taken when the whole or a part of the supplied product batch is found to be non-conforming?

Purchase Processes...

- What extra safeguards are adopted for verification when non-conforming product is submitted after rectification?
- How is the performance of suppliers evaluated? Are the results of evaluation shared with suppliers to enable them to improve?
- Are the suppliers involved in quality improvement projects?
- What steps are taken to encourage long-term relationship with the suppliers?

Production Planning

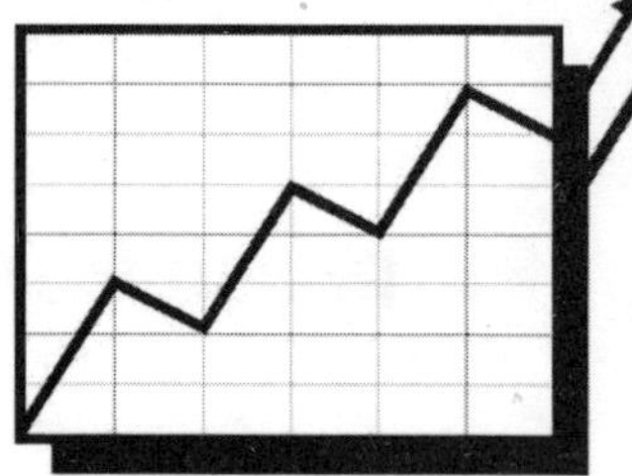

- What is the production policy to ensure that the right quantity of products are produced at the right time to optimize the utilization of production resources?
- What are the inputs to production planning? (These could be confirmed orders, sales forecast and planned inventory levels).
- Is the process capability study conducted for determining the production capacity?

Production Planning...

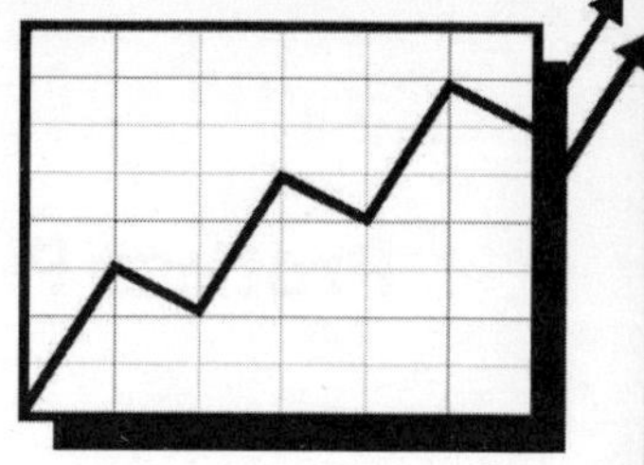

- What is the process of machine loading and work scheduling to ensure smooth flow of production?
- How is production control exercised to ensure that the planned production is achieved?
- Are the causes of production shortfall analyzed to improve the production planning process and productivity?

Process Planning

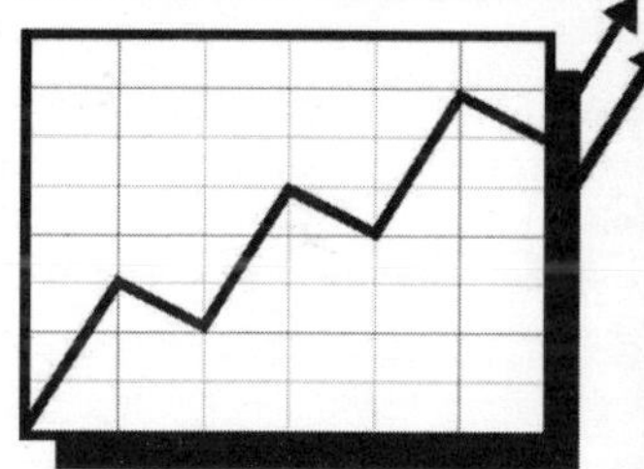

- Has the sequence of operations for each product and the output required at each stage been defined?
- Have the written instructions for various process stages been determined for proper compliance?
- Does the process plan specify the parameters to be checked or measured at different stages and how these measurements are to be carried out?
- Has the criteria for acceptance been defined for each stage along with the actions to be taken in case these criteria are not met?

Process Planning

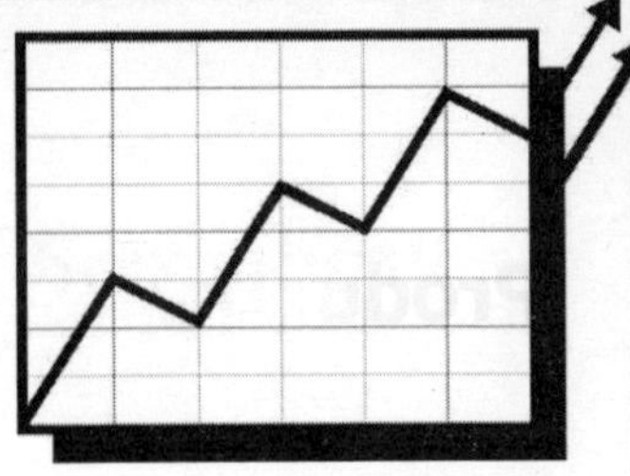

- Does the process plan give details of tooling, software and measuring devices to be used in the process?
- Where a customer-supplied product is to be integrated with the final product, does the process plan provide specifications for such a product and instructions for assessing conformity and related issues?
- Have the methods of identification and traceability been defined?
- Does the process plan contain instructions for preservation, packaging and storage of the product where appropriate?

Production Control

- How it is ensured that the concerned personnel fully understand the process plans and activities to be carried out by them?
- Are all written instructions available at the workstations where ever required?
- What is the method of approval before commencing regular production?
- How is it ensured that the specified process controls are being used and are effective?

Production Control...

- Do the operators know what corrective action is to be taken when a process goes out of control or non-conforming products are produced?
- How it is ensured that an out of control process is not operated until its causes are determined and the corrective action is taken to bring the process back in control?

Production Control...

- What action is to be taken for dealing with non-conforming products?
- What is the process for accepting product deviations that do not significantly affect product serviceability?

Monitoring & Measuring

- Are all monitoring and measuring devices uniquely identified?
- How it is determined that these devices meet the measurement requirements of products and processes?
- Are the calibration procedures documented and are the records of calibration maintained?
- Is calibration status clearly identifiable on the devices?

Monitoring & Measuring...

- Are the concerned personnel aware of proper handling, maintenance and storage method to prevent damage?
- Are suitable environmental conditions maintained for measurement and calibration activities?
- What is the system of re-validation of previous measurements if the measuring equipment is found to be out of calibration?

Process Improvement

- What are the methods for measuring and monitoring product-realization processes?
- Are there records to show that the processes are being monitored and necessary follow-up action is taken to keep them under control?
- Is there a documented plan for inspection and testing before releasing the product?

Process Improvement...

- Is there a documented procedure for control of non-conforming products?
- Are there instructions for the action to be taken when defects are found after delivery and is there an adequate product recall procedure?
- Is there a procedure for corrective and preventive action to prevent occurrence of defects? Does it address the root causes on the basis of investigation and analysis of non-conformities?

Process Improvement...

- Is there a documented procedure for measuring customer satisfaction and handling of customer complaints?
- Are the internal audits carried out according to a plan and the necessary follow-up action taken?
- Are there documented audit procedures along with a check-list?
- Is there a formal system for analysis of data for continuous improvement of processes and quality management system?

7

Innovation

Creativity & Innovation

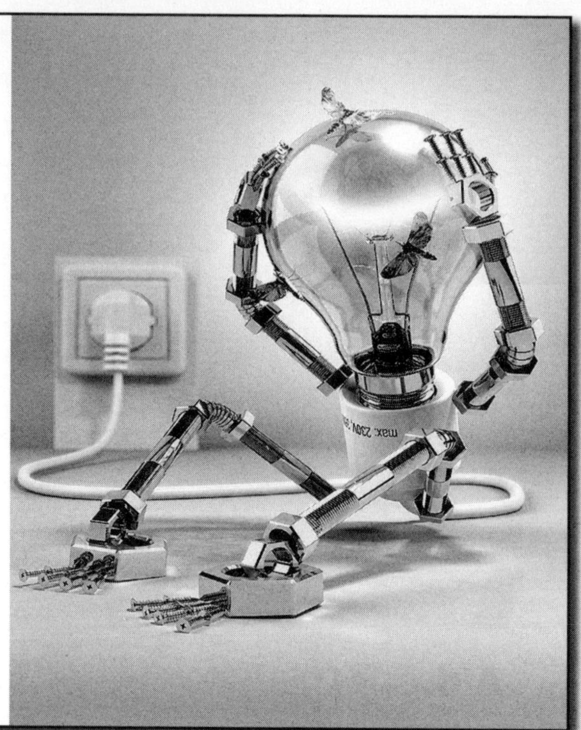

"Innovation distinguishes between a leader and a follower."

Steve Jobs, CEO Apple Computers

A dream with courage is innovation...

IBM

**"The way you will thrive in this environment is by innovating new products, values and business models for meeting untapped customer needs.
Innovation today is about selecting and executing the right ideas and bringing them to market in record time."**

IBM CEO - Samuel J. Palmisano

"Do not go where the path may lead, go instead where there is no path and leave a trail."

Ralph Waldo Emerson

The Most Valuable Differentiator

- Over the last two decades, many companies felt the most surefire way to maintain a competitive advantage in their industry was through quality or price.
- The research at the Ernst & Young Center for Business Innovation (CBI) has revealed, however, that innovation is one of the most valuable differentiators for sustainable competitive advantages.

Creativity & Innovation

Creativity is the ability to produce new and original ideas and things. Innovation **makes the idea practical and usable.** The innovative activity in any business enterprise depends upon the creative contributions of its members.

Relationship between Creativity and Innovation

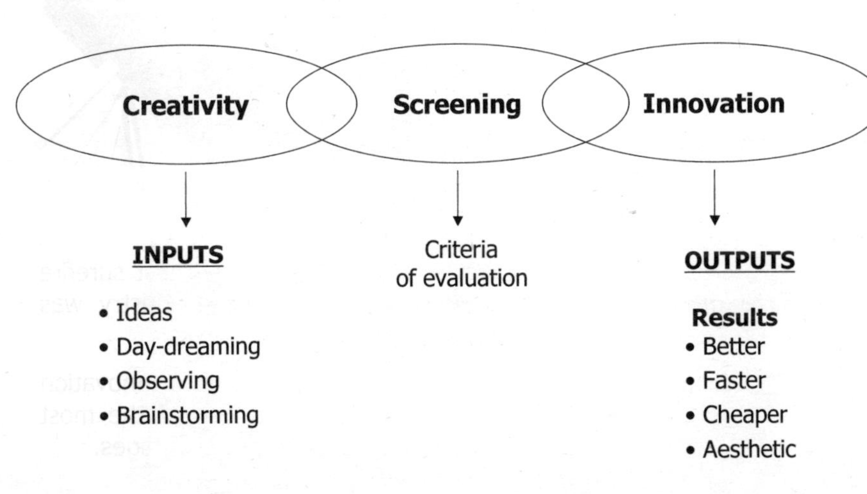

Elements of the Creative Process

The overall creative process has five elements :

1. **Preparation**
2. **Incubation**
3. **Intimation**
4. **Illumination**
5. **Verification**

1. Preparation

This requires proper definition of the problem being faced by the organization.

2. Incubation

Incubation requires partially turning off the process of conventional thinking. This involves holding or keeping in check the normal tendency to criticize and judge the value of what is taking place in the flow of thought. A lot of free thinking without any constraints should be encouraged in the stage.

3. Intimation

In the intimation stage, the person gets some kind of a feeling that he is approaching the solution.

4. Illumination

If incubation is successful, there follows the moment of illumination, which often is like a flash of lightening. The sudden insight of people is linked to a mystical experience. People who have experienced illumination have generally expressed as **"Ah-ha"** effect.

5. Verification

The final stage of creative process is verification. Here the mind returns to the pursuit of more conventional patterns and works out the creative solution in details, polishes it in a more final form, and chooses some test or method of proof so that the idea becomes creditable and accepted.

Challenge the Impossible

It is not unusual to find the birth of a great idea in the minds and words of someone ignorant of the specialized field. Perhaps they don't know enough to know that it can't be done.

'Out-of-the-box' Thinking...

- The bell was invented by an astronomer - **Edmund Halley**
- The pneumatic tyre was invented by veterinarian - **John Dunlop**
- The safety razor was invented by a sales man - **K.C. Gillette**
- The vaccum cleaner was invented by a bridge builder - **Hubert Booth**

Key Principles of Creativity

Principle 1

Produce or bring about something partly or wholly new.

Principle 2

Investigate an existing object with new properties or characteristics.

Principle 3

Imagine new possibilities that were not conceived of before.

Principle 4

Perform something in a manner different from what was thought possible or normal previously.

Developing Creativity

- Give individual brilliance a free hand.
- Nurture passion.
- Encourage 'out-of-the-box' thinking.
- Support their creative initiatives.
- Do not punish failures.

Barriers to Creativity

- Be as practical as you can.
- Follow all the rules.
- That is not logical.
- I am not paid to think.
- Someone else may already be doing it.
- To make a mistake is wrong.
- If I share my ideas someone else may steal.

Innovation is Easy!

Many people think that innovation is a lucky flash of inspiration or a unique skill mastered by fortunate few.

Invention Vs. Innovation

- Invention is discovering things that have never been discovered before.
- Innovation, on the other hand, is the discovery of new ways of creating value. Not everyone can be an inventor, but everyone can be innovative.

Innovation is Easy!

Innovation is looking at NEW WAYS of adding customer value or resolving the critical business problems.

NEW Dimensions to Innovation

- **New What?**
- **New How?**
- **New Why?**
- **New Where?**
- **New When?**
- **New Who?**

New What?

- What are the existing customer problems?
- What are the important areas, which the competition has ignored?
- What are the future needs of the customers in light of the present developments in the market place?
- What are the new opportunities?
- What are the new ideas?
- What are the new product & technology trends?
- What are the new business models?
- What are the new points of differentiation?

New How?

- How else can we address the new customer needs?
- How can we add more value to the customers beyond the industry standards?
- How can we reduce the cost much below the industry standards?
- How can we deliver at much better speed?
- How can we generate new customer needs?
- How can we make it more easier for the customers?
- How can we improve the product design to have 'WOW' factors?

New Why?

- Why do we need this activity?
- Why can't we eliminate these processes?
- Why can't we substitute this with something better?
- Why can't we create a new business model?
- Why can't we outsource?
- Why should we continue like this?
- Why will people buy?
- Why can't we make use of other technologies to resolve the problem?

New Where?

- Where else can we find our resources?
- Where else can we market?
- Where else can we find our new customers?
- Where are the new capabilities?

New When?

- When will our customers need the product?
- When can we address their needs?
- When is the best time to tap the customers?

New Who?

- Who are our new customers?
- Who can we partner with for adding value to customers?
- Who can become our new suppliers?

Look for Unconventional Solutions

For every customer need or a business problem, which cannot be resolved easily through conventional wisdom, there exists an unconventional / unusual solution in the form of innovation.

Find that out!

Innovation Enablers

- Cutting edge manufacturing technology.
- Design softwares.
- Internet & Mobile technology.
- State-of-the-art capabilities.
- Express delivery and logistics.
- Substitute materials.
- Packing technology.
- Automation.
- Retail chains.

Types of Innovation

1. **Products Innovation**
2. **Value Innovation**
3. **Design Innovation**
4. **Process Innovation**
5. **Collaborative Innovation**

"Containerization is a remarkable achievement. No one foresaw how the box would transform everything it touched - from ships and ports to patterns of global trade. Containerization is a monument to the most powerful law in economics, that of unanticipated consequences."

Marc Levinson, author of **The Box -** How the shipping container made the world smaller and the world economy bigger.

Products Innovation...

Coming up with absolutely **New products or services** for the customers. This is also known as customer inspired innovation that often transforms the market and industries and helps in generating quantum jumps in revenues.

Customer Insight

Customer insight represents a deep understanding of customer needs and the drivers of customer behaviour at a levels, well beyond 'what the customers are able to articulate themselves'.

Customer insight leads to opportunities for creating solutions that are tightly linked to the core drivers of human needs and behaviour.

Customer Insight...

Developing Customer Insight includes:

Understanding the explicitly stated or 'articulated' needs of customers and potential customers, but more significantly identifying their **'unarticulated' & unperceived needs.**

Customer Inspired

Customer inspired innovation is the imaginative discovery of new products & services by matching deep insight into customer needs with an organization's capabilities in unprecedented ways.

Articulated Customer Needs

- 'Articulated Customer Needs' are needs that are recognized and communicated by customers.
- These needs are often short-term focused.
- They lead only to incremental opportunities.

Unarticulated Customer Needs

'Unarticulated Customer Needs' are the needs unrecognized by customers. These needs often lead to breakthrough opportunities. They have the maximum potential to change the basis of competition, transform an industry and create whole new solution.

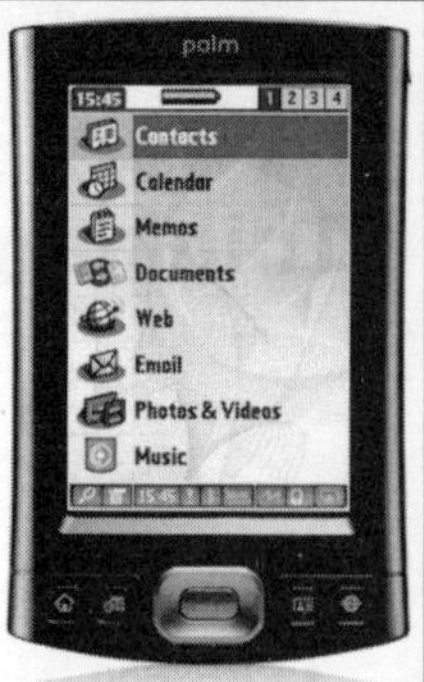

Principles

- Envision the future dramatically different from the present.
- Engage the customer as a collaborator, partner and knowledge resource – an integral part of the product development process.
- Challenge the business boundaries and explore beyond the existing comfort zones – where breakthroughs reside. Few examples are given below.

'Driver-less' Cars by Volkswagen

- The Volkswagen Passat drives using two eye-like laser sensors in the front and one in the back that scan road conditions, buildings, other vehicles and pedestrians over a range of up to 200 meters (650 feet).
- An on-board computer digests and acts on the information using software developed by the Germany-based Ibeo Automobile Sensor company.

Thinking Chair

- Research found that most users rarely bother adjusting the complex controls found on the work chairs and that work surfaces often conflict with the chair arms, forcing users into poorly supported postures. This innovative chair 'thinks' for the person sitting on it.
- It automatically adjusts the tension of the back support and moves fluidly with the body, providing support in proportion to the body weight. The chair can also support an optional headrest and adjustable lumbar support. In addition to conventional adjustments for height and pivot, the arms can retract front to back bringing workers closer to their work.

Safety Vocal Smoke Detector

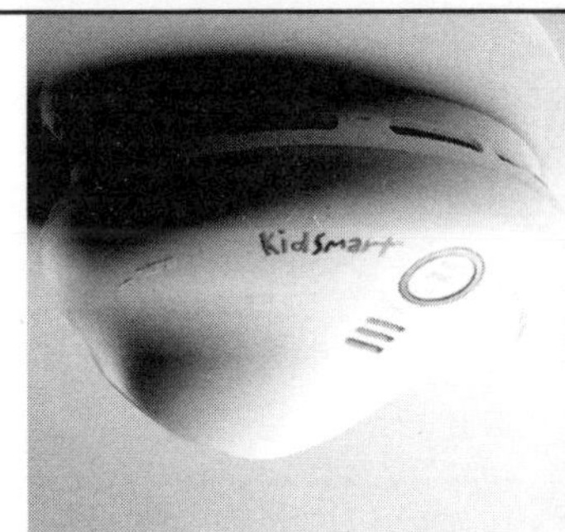

- The safety 'Vocal Smoke Detector' (VSD) uses a parent's recorded voice to wake children in case of a fire and provides them with evacuation instructions.
- The VSD is effective in waking nearly twice as many sleeping children as traditional smoke alarms. The device's interface makes it easy for parents to record the voice alarm message through a combination of written directions and step-by-step verbal prompts.

Bumpbrella

- The Bumpbrella is a fresh, innovative exploration of a ubiquitous product: the umbrella. To open the umbrella, an integrated bicycle pump housed in the handle inflates the decorative, transparent vinyl.
- Once inflated, users can better see their surroundings and avoid collisions with other umbrellas or obstacles.
- Adding a touch of fun, three high-output LEDs illuminate decorative markings on the vinyl. When the sun comes out, simply turn the handle backwards to deflate the umbrella.

GlowBouy

- The GlowBouy is a battery powered, floating swimming pool light powerful enough to illuminate an average size pool. It offers an affordable alternative to permanently installed pool lights and adds a warm ambient glow to night time swimming.
- Its uniform 360-degree design refracts light evenly throughout the pool, eliminating the shadows and dark spots inherent with wall pool lights. The design is also easy to use - just turn it on and throw it in the pool. The soft top, rounded shapes and color were drawn from aquatic plants and animals for a friendly appeal.

Beyond Customers

The customer insight approach is not restricted to customers but often involves other stakeholders in the value chain:

- Channel partners
- Suppliers
- Manufacturing partners
- Other potential alliance partners
- Employees
- Media
- Investors

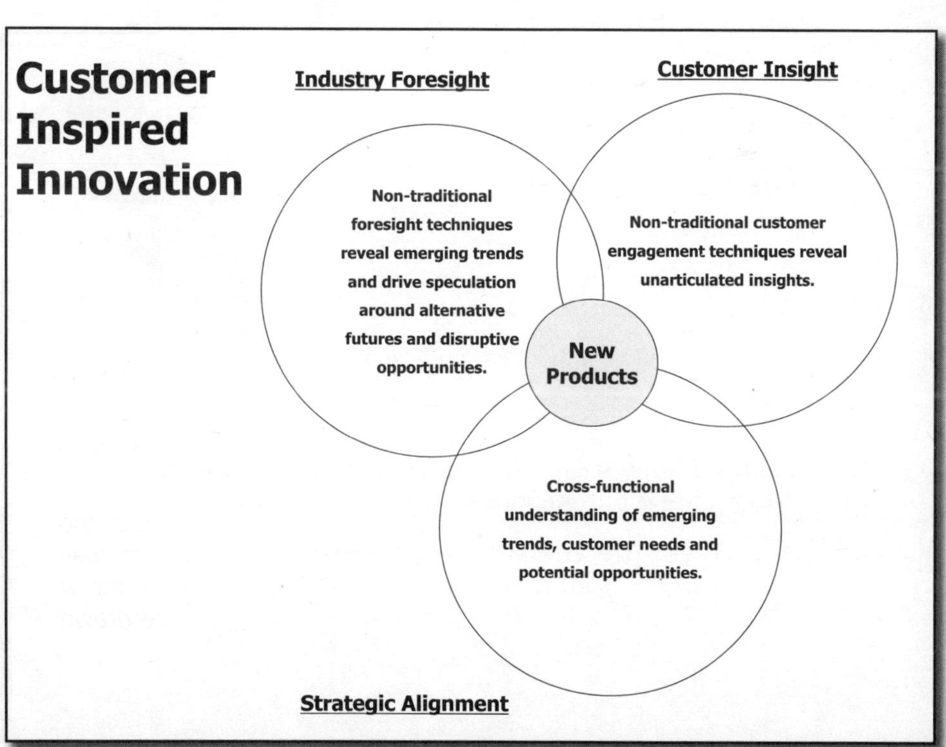

2. Value Innovation

Value Innovation

This involves adding NEW VALUES by taking into consideration the multiple dimensions of product performance.

Value Innovation...

- Wal-Mart, Pantaloon & Mcdonald continue to grow profitably through aggressive volume, pricing and delivery offerings to customers.
- Nokia bundles internet, emailing, music and camera with their mobile phones to maximize value to customers.
- GOOGLE provides fastest search on text, images, videos, maps and softwares.

Value Innovation...

- There are hundreds of **permutations and combinations** for maximizing customer value - features, functions, services, choice, price range, combined offers, customer experience, delivery etc.
- Value innovations are the **best kept secrets** of successful organizations and are going to play the most important role for sustained competitive advantages.

Successful Value Innovation

- Think of yourself as a **provider of solutions,** rather than of products or services.
- Distinguish between what you are selling and **what your customer is buying.**
- Take a broad view of your **customer's underlying problems** that go beyond you and your products.
- Price in **terms of value** rather than cost.

Design Innovation

This involves coming up with absolutely **NEW DESIGN** in the products to make an impact on the customers. Great designs rule every where - Consumer electronics, automobiles, consumer durables & non-durables, architecture, retail and fashion.

Design – the Differentiator

All Equal Except ...

"At Sony we assume that all products of our competitors have basically the same technology, price, performance and features. Design is the only thing that differentiates one product from another in the marketplace."

Norio Ohga

'WOW' Factors

Consumers who are choking on choice, look at design as the new differentiator.

Stiff Competition

- In the fast changing world, today's breakthrough design is tomorrow's undifferentiated commodity.
- What was once thought of as a great design, is now merely seen as 'good' and what was once considered as an exceptional design, is now just a mandatory standard.

Components of Design Excellence

- Aesthetics – Wow factors
- Uncommon / Different / Stands out
- Blend of craftsmanship & performance
- Creative
- Ergonomics aspects
- User-friendly
- Futuristic looks
- Attention to fine details

4. Process Innovation

Process Innovation

- This requires coming up with new processes that maximize **speed, service and quality.**
- ATM machines save lot of customer's and bank's time.
- On-line air reservations save lot of customer's and airline's time.

Process Innovation...

Apart from cash withdrawals, customers are being offered the following additional services from the bank's ATM:

- Shop for a housing loan.
- Make donations to temple.
- Pay college fees.
- Pay telephone bills.
- Pay LIC premiums.
- Invest in mutual funds.
- Book train / air tickets.
- Transfer money across the country / globally.

Process Innovation...

You can pick up the key business processes that offer maximum value propositions to your customers and re-engineer them so that they deliver speed, service, quality and **SIMPLICITY.**

5. Collaborative Innovation

Collaborative Innovation

This requires finding new synergies and connecting with other organizations for mutual benefits. Organizations that harness the creativity and capabilities of many other organizations, can make better products for greater customer values.

Collaborative Innovation...

- Consumer goods company Sara Lee realized that its core competencies were in consumer insight, brand management, marketing and distribution. Thus, it divested itself of a majority of its manufacturing operations and formed alliances with manufacturing and supply chain partners.
- The same applies to Nike and Reebok who concentrate mainly on marketing & retailing.

Look for Synergy

- Think of those areas where your organization's strength is another company's major challenge and form innovative collaborations for mutual benefits.
- Look for mutually advantageous partnerships where the **whole is greater than the sum of the parts.**

Integrating Capabilities

ORGANIZATION:1		ORGANIZATION:2
Manufacturing	→	Marketing
Product	←	Brand
Customer base	→	Technical capabilities
Supply chain	←	Retail chain
Intellectual strengths	→	Financial strengths

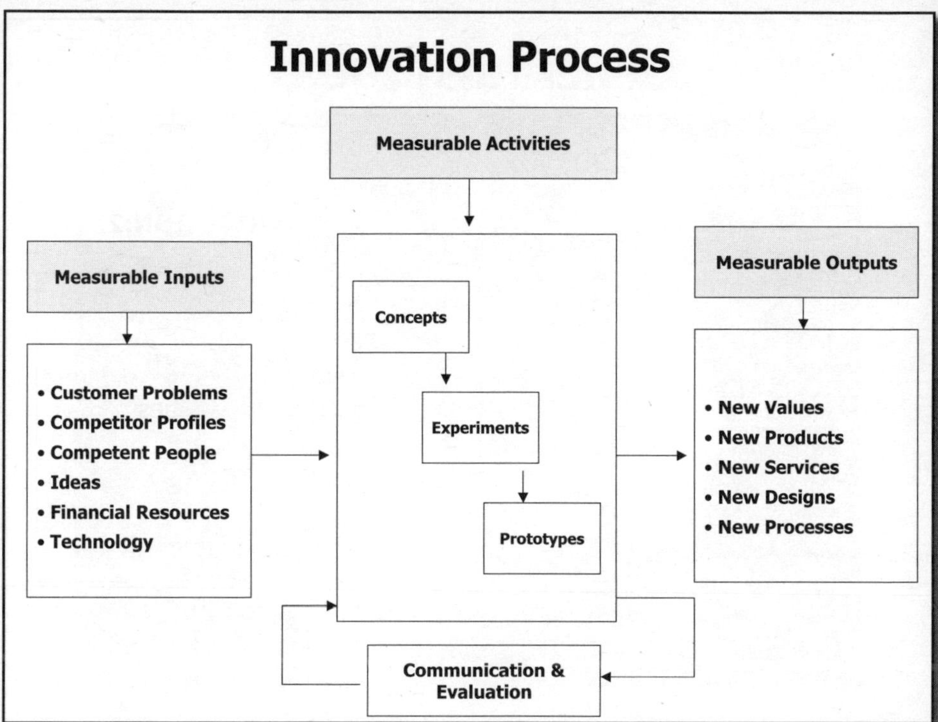
Innovation Process
Measurable Activities
Measurable Inputs
• Customer Problems
• Competitor Profiles
• Competent People
• Ideas
• Financial Resources
• Technology
Concepts
Experiments
Prototypes
Measurable Outputs
• New Values
• New Products
• New Services
• New Designs
• New Processes
Communication & Evaluation

Generating Ideas

"There is one thing stronger than all the armies in the world, and that is an

IDEA

whose time has come."

Victor Hugo

"Aviation is a proof that given the will, we can do the impossible."
Eddie Rickenbacker

"Life is the application of noble and profound ideas to life."

Matthew Arnold

Learning from the Genius

It will be interesting to go deep into the mind of Thomas Edison and take lessons from one of the greatest minds of our time. The man had no formal educational background, but holds the world record of more than 1000 patents. Some of his words are timeless treasures that still hold a great potential for innovation:

- "Diamond is a coal that stuck to its job."
- "The three things that are most essential to achievement are common sense, hard work and stick-to-it-iv-ness."
- "Opportunity is missed by most people because it is dressed in overalls and looks like work."

Generating Ideas

Ideas are the raw material for innovation and the progress of any nation. The human capacity to contemplate the ideas is associated with the capacity to reason, self-reflection and the ability to acquire and apply intellect.

Ideas give rise to concepts, which are the basis for any kind of knowledge - whether science or philosophy. Important sources of business ideas are given below.

1. Existing Problems

Every problem presents a great opportunity to innovate. Successful innovation requires a deeper understanding of the problems and customer insights. Few examples of great innovations emerging from the problems are given below:

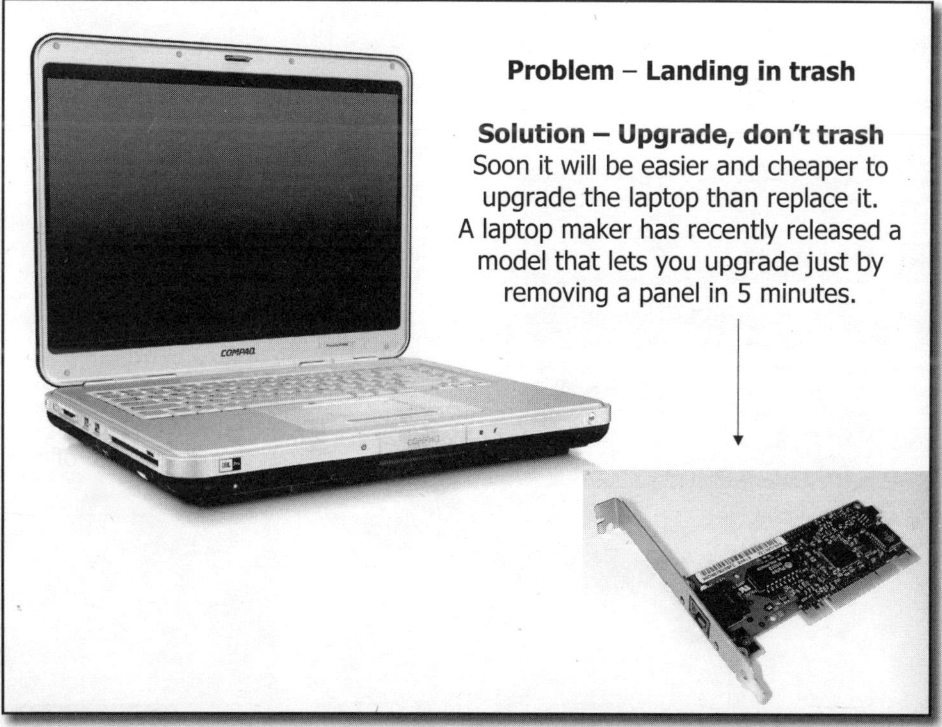

Problem – Petroleum based plastic

Solution – Corn based plastic
New corn bases bio-plastics require less energy to produce than the traditional plastics.

Problem – Power sucking displays

Solution – Create better displays
An LCD can consume more than half of a laptop's power due to fluorescent backlight. The solution is to use self-luminescent OLEDs (new technology) made from organic chemicals, which consume less power.

Problem – Hard drive

Solution – Flash drive
Future lap tops can knock off energy consumption by replacing hard drives with flash drives.

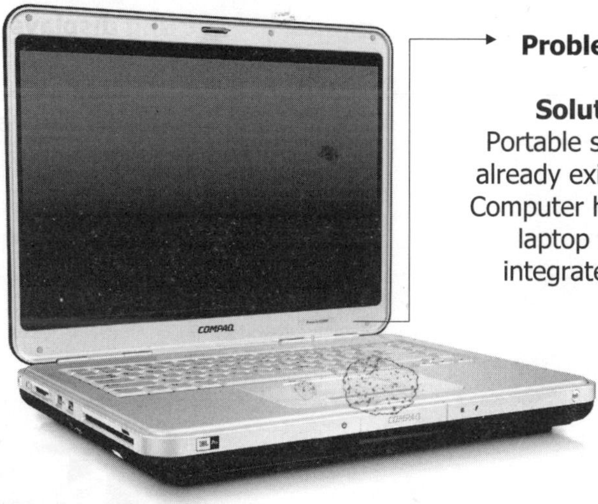

Problem – Battery power

Solution – Solar power
Portable solar chargers for laptops already exist. A company called MSI Computer has developed a prototype laptop with photovoltaic cells integrated directly into its case.

Internet Story

Tim Berner Lee found it frustrating that during earlier days, there was different information on various computers and one had to log on to different computers to get the desired information. Sometimes he had to learn different programs on each computer. Therefore, finding out how things worked was really difficult and cumbersome for him.

According to Tim Berner Lee "when you are a programmer and you solve a problem and then you solve another one that is very similar, you often think:

- Isn't there a better way?
- Can't we just fix this problem for good?
- Can't we develop a program easily accessible to all?"

This ultimately resulted in the discovery of HTML and internet, which has completely revolutionised the way we work and conduct our business.

Google Story

Larry Page and Sergi Brin, the co-founders of Google realized that computing's biggest challenge was retrieving relevant information from the massive set of data. They converted this into a great business opportunity by developing the fastest search engine.

Google is the greatest innovation success story of our times. Google gets 2.5 billion hits to its search engine every day.

Nestle Story

In the 1860s Henri Nestle a pharmacist, developed a food for babies who were unable to breastfeed. His first success was a premature infant who could not tolerate his mother's milk or any of the usual substitutes. People quickly recognized the value of the new product, after Nestle's new formula saved the child's life - the rest is a history. Nestle is the global leader in food products.

2. Imagination

**"You see things and say why?
I dream of things and say
Why not?"**

George Bernard Shaw

Imagination...

Man's imagination has lit up every lamp in this world, made it possible for the man fly in air, reach the depths of ocean, brought the world on the fingertips through internet, made every single discovery and created wonderful products for better living on this planet. Man is still not satisfied. His imagination is now exploring the possibilities of exploring life on moon and other planets.

Imagination...

Man's brain is the greatest natural resource in this world and imagination is the priceless ingredient for the mankind's progress in future. It is a creative faculty and the ability to fantasize. The history of the business is essentially the history of imagination. Nothing is impossible, there are ways that lead to the desired end and the means always follow.

Imagination...

A powerful imagination makes us infinite; in fact it is quite often an excuse when we say that this is not possible. We should instead ask, why is this not possible?

3. Brainstorming

- Brainstorming is an effective way of developing ideas. It is a **'group creativity technique'** designed to generate a large number of ideas for the solution to a problem.
- It works by focusing on a problem and then coming up with many radical solutions to it. Ideas should deliberately be kept as broad and odd as possible and should be developed as fast as possible.
- Brainstorming is a lateral thinking process, which helps in breaking our thinking patterns into new ways of looking at things.

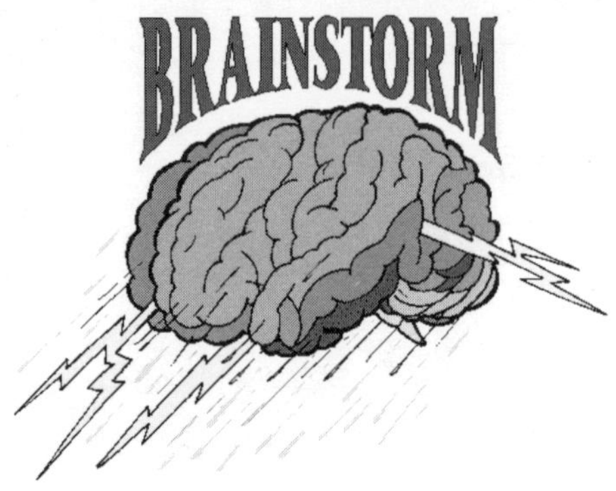

During brainstorming sessions there should be no criticism of ideas. The objective of brainstorming is to open new possibilities and break down the wrong assumptions about the limits of a particular problem. Judgment and analysis at this stage will hinder the idea generation. Ideas should only be evaluated once the brainstorming session has concluded.

Brainstorming Process

1. Present the problem and give a further explanation if needed.
2. Ask the brainstorming participants for their ideas.
3. Suggest a lead to encourage creativity.
4. Allow each participant to present his or her idea.
5. Elaborate on the idea to improve the quality.
6. Organize the ideas based on the goal and encourage discussions.
7. Generate additional ideas if required.
8. Categorize the ideas.
9. Review the ideas to ensure that everyone understands them.
10. Evaluate and select the best idea.

4. Customers

No one can provide you with the better ideas than your customers. Sit with them, talk to them, engage them in new product developments, visit them and ask them for ideas. Put yourself into their shoes. Think of their future needs.

Continuous Customer Feedback

- Listen to the customers continuously and not at discreet intervals.
- Keep comment cards at high volume locations.
- Use feedback to identify new segments and customer expectations.
- Design varying customer listening devices for different needs.
- Convert every point of customer interaction into a listening point.
- Listen to customers at 'moments of truth'. For example, settlement of insurance claim and getting a loan from the bank.

Ask Customers for Their Wish List

Few Examples

- Sprinklers that will automatically wash the car.
- A tracking device, which can track the children so that they don't get lost in the markets or public places.
- Automatic food makers that will make the food of your choice.
- Cars with auto sensors or repulsive magnetic pulls so that they never crash with each other.
- Cars fitted with tyres, which will never get flat. When we are making such expensive cars, why not have solid rubber tyres?

5. Suppliers

Some times great ideas can come from your suppliers. Suppliers can provide important information that could lead to breakthroughs in design, product substitutions, alternative technology etc.

6. Passionate Employees

Turn to the most passionate & creative people in your organization. Many people still confuse innovation with R&D, R&D with labs and labs with millions of dollars investment.

Great works are the result of great passions. **Microsoft and Hewlett Packard** are excellent examples, which have emerged from the garage and not from any R&D labs.

7. External Environment

The day to day developments in the world of business, science, govt. policies, stock market trends, magazines, journals, publications, internet, current affairs and competition can provide lot of business ideas for innovation.

Microsoft Story

In December 1974, Paul Allen was on his way to visit Bill Gates, when along the way he stopped to browse the current magazines. What he saw changed his and Bill Gates's lives for ever. On the cover of Popular Electronics was a picture of the Altair 8080 and the headline "World's First Microcomputer Kit to rival commercial models." He bought the issue and rushed over to Bill Gates. They both recognized this as their big opportunity.

Microsoft Story...

The two knew that the home computer market was about to explode and that someone would need to make software for the new machines. Within a few days, Gates had called MITS (Micro Instrumentation and Telemetry Systems), the makers of the Altair. He told the company that he and Allen had developed a BASIC that could be used on the Altair. MITS arranged a deal with Gates and Allen to buy the rights of their BASIC. Gates was convinced that the software market had been born and the rest is a history.

TRIZ

- TRIZ is the Russian Acronym for **"Teoriya Resheniya Izobretatelskikh Zadatch"** – A theory of solving inventive problems.
- The methodology was developed by Soviet engineer and researcher Genrich Saulovich Altshuller while working at the "Inventions Inspection" department. He reviewed about 40,000 patent abstracts, in order to find out the ways in which innovation had taken place. He eventually developed 40 principles of invention.

TRIZ...

TRIZ is a methodology and model-based technology for generating innovative ideas and solutions for problem solving. TRIZ provides tools and methods for use in problem formulation, system analysis, failure analysis and patterns of system evolution. Some of the important TRIZ principles are given below.

Apply these principles for successful innovation...

1. Segmentation

Divide an object into independent parts.

Examples

- Replace a large truck by a container.
- Modular furniture.

2. Taking Out

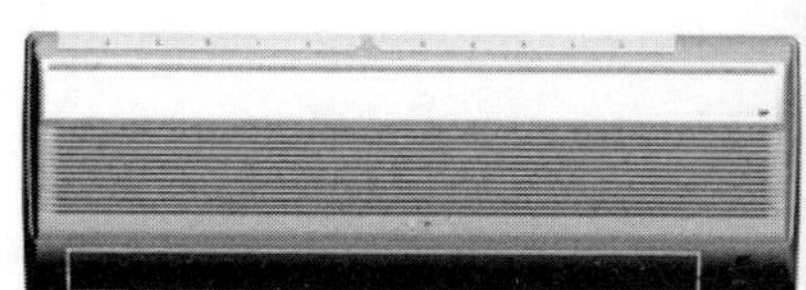

Separate an interfering part or property from an object, or single out the only necessary part of an object.

Example

Split A.C uses different areas for chilling and different for compressor.

3. Quality Features

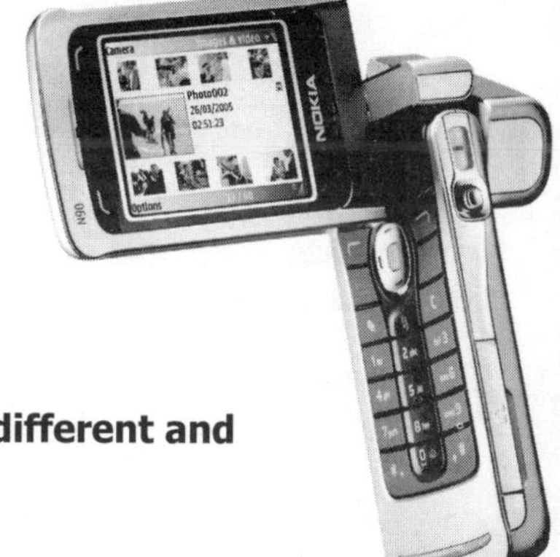

Make each part of an object fulfill a different and useful function.

Examples

- Mobile phone as camera.
- DVD players as radio and music systems.

4. Asymmetry

Change the shape of an object from symmetrical to asymmetrical.

Examples

- Mixers
- Blenders
- Cement mixing trucks

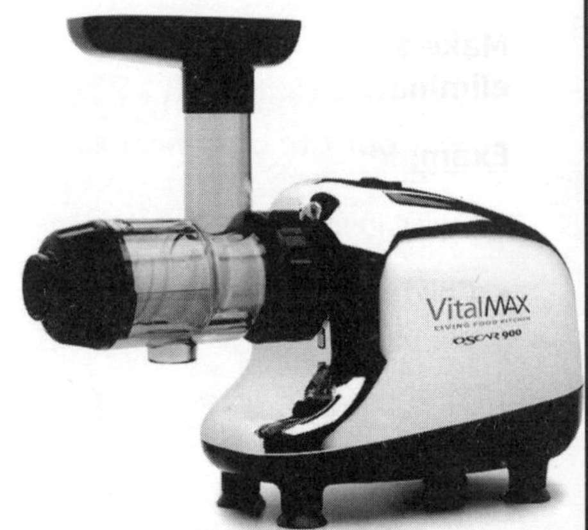

5. Merging

Bring closer identical or similar objects, assemble identical or similar parts to perform parallel operations.

Examples

- Phones with internet interface.
- Computers with T.V interface.
- Mobile phones with music.

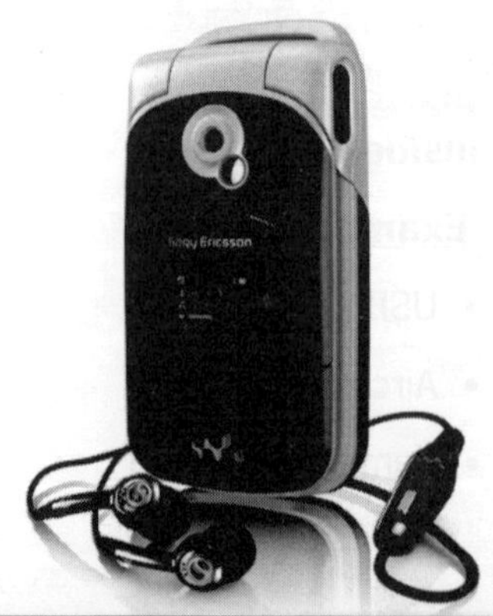

6. Universality

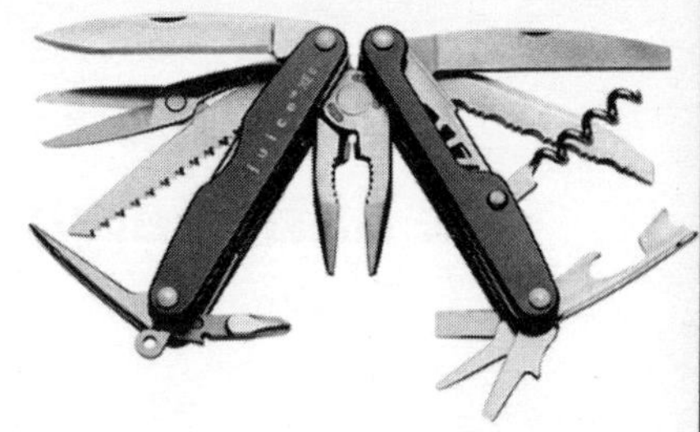

Make a part or object to perform the multiple functions and eliminate the need for other parts.

Examples

- Swiss knife can perform multiple functions.
- Child's car safety seat converts to a stroller.

7. Nested Doll

Place one object inside another. Place each object, in turn, inside the other.

Examples

- USB port of a cordless mouse can fit into the mouse.
- Aircraft entertainment systems rest on the back side of the seats.
- Camera zoom lens.

8. Anti-weight

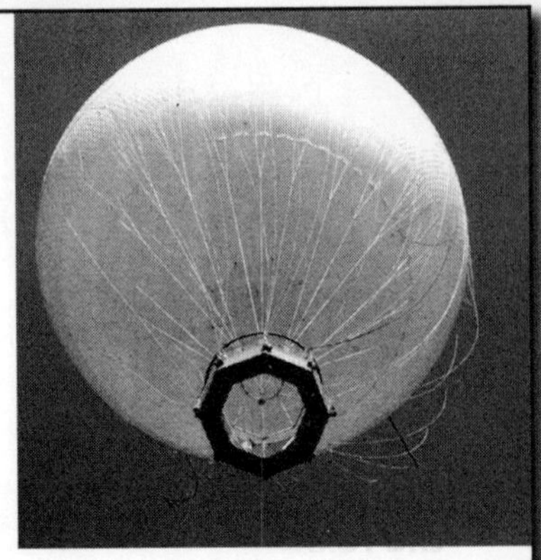

To compensate for the weight of an object, merge it with other objects that provide lift.

Example

Helium balloon is used at Niagara Falls for giving bird's eye view to the tourists.

9. Combining Technologies

Combining different technologies to produce new results.

Example

- Automobiles with computer navigation controls.

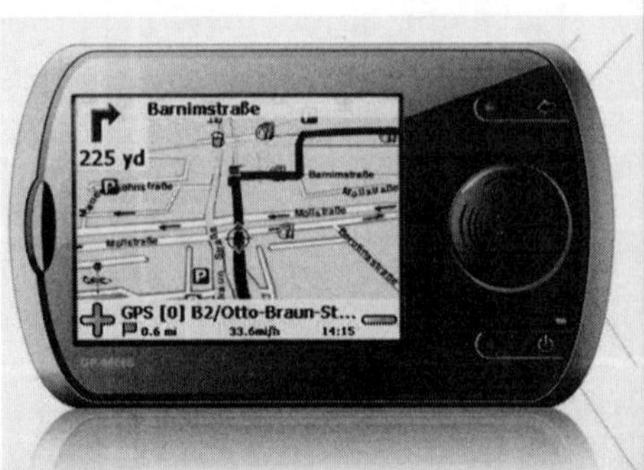

10. Contingency Aspect

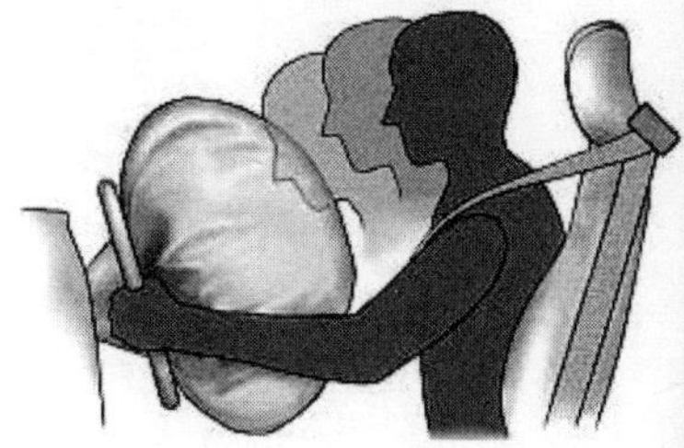

Prepare emergency means beforehand to compensate for the relatively low reliability.

Examples

- Alternative engines in aircrafts.
- Cars with airbags to prevent injury to the passengers.
- Power back-ups for PCs.

11. Eliminating

Eliminate standard operations to increase speed, service and quality.

Examples

- ATM machines.
- Vending machines.

12. Reverse / The other way round

Invert the action(s) used to solve the problem.

Examples

- Moving sidewalks on airport.
- Tread mill.
- Mobile clinics.

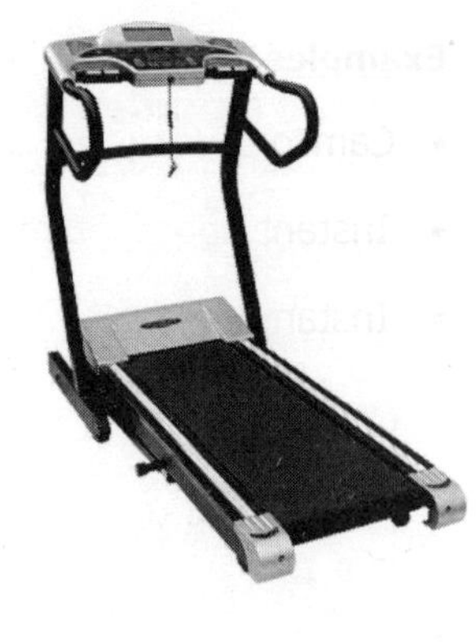

13. Substitute

Substitute materials to save time, cost and money.

Examples

- Credit / debit cards for paper money.
- Glass for bricks in architecture.
- Plastic for wooden furniture.

14. Instant Action

This requires integrating various technologies to produce instant results.

Examples

- Camcorders make instant DVDs.
- Instant photographs.
- Instant tea / coffee.

15. New Dimension

To move an object in two or three dimensional space.

Examples

- Infrared computer mouse moves in space, instead of a surface.
- Both sides of the sign board can be used for display.
- Multi-layer parking systems.

16. Mechanical Vibration

Use vibrations to perform functions.

Examples:

- Destroy kidney stones using ultrasonic vibrations.
- Mobile phones vibrate to signal incoming calls.

17. Blessing in Disguise

Use harmful factors to achieve a positive effect.

Examples:

- Use wind currents to generate electric power.
- Use sugarcane molasses for producing ethanol – A bio fuel.
- Use bio-degradable garbage as fertilizers.

18. Feedback Mechanism

Introduce feedback to improve a process or action.

Examples

- Radars for aircraft monitoring.
- CCTV cameras replace people for vigilance.
- Alarms in automatic surveillance systems.

19. Self-service

Make an object serve itself.

Examples

- Driverless cars by Volkswagen.
- Driverless trains at the airports of Orlando and New York.

20. Cheap Short-living Objects

Replace an expensive object with multiple and inexpensive objects.

Examples

- Throw away razors.
- Disposable syringe.

"The experienced mountain climber is not intimidated by a mountain - he is inspired by it. The persistent winner is not discouraged by a problem - he is challenged by it. Mountains are created to be conquered; adversities are designed to be defeated; problems are sent to be solved. It is better to master one mountain than a thousand foothills."

William Arthur Ward

IDEAS

Ideas and imagination are the raw material or the starting point for innovation.

NEW QUESTIONS

Innovation starts with asking new WHAT?, new WHO?, new HOW?, new WHERE?, new WHEN? and new WHY?

INNOVATION

NEW CUSTOMER NEEDS

Translate unperceived and unarticulated customer needs into development of new products and services.

INNOVATION

OBSTACLES

Look at the existing obstacles and problems for successful innovation. All great innovations begin with obstacles and problems. Think of resolving the problems in an unconventional manner.

I N N O V A T I O N

VALUES

Customer value enrichment is the basis of all innovation. Think of ways in which customer values can be maximized and new values can be created. Value innovations are the best kept secrets of leading organizations.

I N N O V A T I O N

ACTION

Ideas must be converted into actions. An ordinary idea which is put to action is far better than a great idea which is only in the mind.

INNOVATION

TECHNOLOGY

Innovation becomes easier by using the existing technologies.

INNOVATION

INTEGRATION

Quite often innovation is the result of integration. Integrate existing products, features, technologies and various disciplines for successful innovation.

INNOVATION

'OUT-OF-THE-BOX' THINKING

Challenge the conventional wisdom and all the existing paradigms. Think opposite, think metaphorically, have the capacity to perceive resemblances between two separate areas, formulate incongruent and unusual combinations, apply non-linear or lateral thinking for out-of-the-box solutions.

INNOVATIO

NEW PRODUCTS & SERVICES

This is the ultimate goal of innovation. The new products and services must be a 'game changer'. It must change the rules of the industry.